Design History

After the First World War, the major naval powers of Great Britain, the USA, Japan, France and Italy, attempted to limit re-armament and any potential future naval arms race by a series of agreements. The Washington Treaty of 1922 restricted cruiser size to 10,000 tons and 8in guns, and countries immediately started building to the maximum size permitted. The Royal Navy, for example, produced the very successful 'County' class (ShipCraft 19) of thirteen vessels.

However, the London Treaty of 1930 went further by defining two different types of cruiser: 'heavy' cruisers with guns larger than 6.1in and 'light' cruisers with guns smaller than 6.1in. The total tonnage for each type was also agreed; in the case of Great Britain it was 146,800 tons for 'heavy' cruisers and 192,200 tons for 'light' cruisers.

Irrespective of any treaty limitations on numbers, Great Britain soon realised it could not afford to keep building such large vessels if it was to reach the number of cruisers deemed necessary. It was also felt that such large cruisers were not ideal for fleet work, and smaller, more manoeuvrable vessels were needed. The initial outcome was a number of light cruiser designs, the first three classes being built with just eight or six 6in guns in twin turrets (ShipCraft 30).

However, other navies began to build light cruisers with more guns. For example, the Japanese had built the *Mogami* class with fifteen 6.1in guns and the USA responded by building the *Brooklyn* class with fifteen 6in guns. To achieve these numbers of guns, it was necessary to utilise triple turrets, and so Great Britain designed the 'Town' (*Southampton/Gloucester/Edinburgh*) and 'Colony' (*Fiji/Uganda*) classes with twelve 6in Mk XXIII guns. These were the same guns as used in the preceding classes, but now installed in Mk XXII or Mk XXIII mountings. Quadruple mountings were also considered, and the remote powered RP10 Mk XXIV mountings were intended for use aboard the later *Tiger* class, but the construction of these was suspended at the end of the war. This design was modified and they eventually completed with twin 6in turrets, to a new and much more powerful design.

SOUTHAMPTON CLASS

With an increase in the number of guns, came the inevitable increase in size – and cost! The design was approved by the

This photograph of *Glasgow* was taken in May 1939, and clearly shows the knuckle at the bow.

The two starboard twin 4in anti-aircraft gun mountings on board *Newcastle* in July 1937.

Admiralty Board on 9 November 1933. The first two ships, *Southampton* and *Newcastle*, were ordered in the 1933 programme, and the others, *Glasgow*, *Birmingham* and *Sheffield*, in the 1934 programme.

The *Southampton* class had a standard displacement of approximately 9000 tons, 2000 tons greater than the preceding classes, an overall length of 591ft 6in, 30ft longer, and a beam of 61ft 8in at the waterline, 5ft greater. The design speed remained the same at 32kts standard. They retained a similar machinery arrangement of Parson's geared turbines driving four shafts, but these were fed by four Admiralty 3-drum boilers, producing 75,000shp. The forward two boilers were arranged in parallel, immediately below the forward funnel, and the aft two were arranged in tandem, below the aft funnel. The two engine rooms were located immediately aft of each boiler room, the forward engine room driving the outer shafts and the aft engine room driving the inner shafts. Endurance was 8900 miles at 16kts. Electrical power was generated by two 300kW turbo-generators, located in the two engine rooms, and two 300kW diesel generators, in separate compartments, to port and starboard of the aft boiler room.

The 6in guns were of the Mk XXIII,

The forward superstructure of *Sheffield*, as seen from aft, in October 1937. Note the stowage of the carley floats between the hangar doors.

breech loading type. The *Southampton* class were fitted with four Mk XXII, triple, short trunk turrets, which had an elevation range of -5° to +45°, with a preferred loading elevation of approximately 6°. The trunnions of the cradle for the centre gun were set back 30in to reduce shell interference. The gunlayer usually followed the director's pointer by hand, power only being used for large movements. Each turret had a magazine and handing room, and duplex electric endless-chain hoists that could deliver shells and charges at a maximum rate of 32 per minute. The charges were delivered to the upper handing room, which was one deck below the gunhouse floor. They were then passed to the cordite gallery, carried by hand round the gallery and passed up 5ft to the revolving structure, and then by hand-ups to the gunhouse.

The shell room was on the same level as the magazine and the fixed shell handing room immediately below the working chamber. Platforms in the shell handling room were attached to the hoists and revolved with them, the shells being fed from a circular chute, which in turn was fed from the lower hoists. The turret shields were 1in thick. 'X' turret was removed from the class in 1944–45, to compensate for the topweight of wartime additions.

The 6in guns' primary control was a revolving Director Control Tower (DCT), with a 15ft rangefinder, fitted on the bridge roof. There was an Admiralty Fire Control Table Mk V. The table had no provision for a second DCT, so a fixed control position was located on the aft superstructure. The 1934 programme vessels received a few small improvements to their fire control arrangements, including a Mk VI fire control table.

Secondary armament consisted of the 4in Mk VI gun in four twin Mk XIX mountings, with an elevation of -10° to +80°, firing at a maximum rate of five rounds per minute. These were sited amidships, aft of the second funnel. A High Angle Director (HACS) was fitted to port and starboard of the forward funnel for their control in *Southampton* and *Newcastle*, a third HACS also being fitted on the centreline aft in the other three.

There were also two quadruple 2pdr pom-pom mountings, consisting of Mk VIII guns on Mk VII mountings, located alongside the forward funnel, two quadruple 0.5in machine gun mountings, consisting of Mk III guns on Mk II mountings, alongside the main mast, and four 3pdr Mk I Hotchkiss saluting guns. Torpedo armament comprised two triple Mk IV* torpedo tubes with Mk IX or IX* torpedoes. The prototype Asdic Type 132 was trialled on *Southampton* in May 1938, and *Sheffield* and *Glasgow* received similar sets by the beginning of the war. All members of the class carried a depth charge rail for a maximum of six depth charges on the port quarter.

SOUTHAMPTON CLASS BUILDING DATA

Name	Builder	Laid down	Launched
Newcastle	Vickers-Armstrong	04.10.1934	23.01.1936
Southampton	John Brown	21.11.1934	10.03.1936
Sheffield	Vickers-Armstrong	31.01.1935	23.07.1936
Glasgow	Scotts	16.04.1935	20.06.1936
Birmingham	Devonport Dyd	18.07.1935	01.09.1936

The different shape of *Birmingham*'s bow, with no knuckle, is immediately obvious in this photograph, taken in February 1938.

The class had a knuckle bow, apart from *Birmingham*; this experiment was not judged a success, but war intervened before the bow could be rebuilt.

The main armour belt was of 4½in, or 180 lbs, cemented armour and protected both engine and boiler rooms, stretching from frame 65, just aft of 'B' turret, to frame 198, just forward of 'X' turret. It was sealed at both ends by 100 lbs non-cemented bulkheads.

The class were intended to carry three Walrus aircraft, two in the hangars sited either side of the forward funnel and a third on the catapult, but this last was rarely (if ever) carried. The catapult was a fixed, reversible, transverse type D1H, with a maximum length of 92ft, capable of launching the Walrus at 56 knots. Two electric cranes were sited aft of the catapult, either side of the aft funnel, and were used to recover the aircraft, and to launch and recover boats. *Sheffield* did not have her catapult fitted until May 1938. The catapults were removed from all members of the class by the end of 1944.

The intended boat outfit comprised two 35ft motor pinnaces, one 36ft motor and pulling pinnace, two 32ft cutters, one 30ft gig and two 27ft whalers. Flagships were to be fitted with a 35ft motor barge, and a 16ft dinghy carried for recreational purposes. In practice this outfit was not always carried, although the 36ft pinnace, 35ft motor boats, 32ft cutters and 27ft whalers were almost always shipped. Close examination of dated photographs is required for complete accuracy. The whalers were carried on quadrantal davits, either side of

This photograph of *Manchester* in 1938 clearly shows the curved front to the bridge.

the aft funnel, and the motor boats were stowed just aft of the funnel, between the twin 4in gun mounts.

The number, size and location of carley floats was continuously changing. Photographs show them stowed on the sides of the main turrets, on the sides of the superstructure, and against the funnel, between the hangars, amongst other locations.

Peacetime complement was approximately 750, between 30% and 50% larger than that of the previous classes of light cruiser.

GLOUCESTER CLASS

The primary consideration for the three 1935 programme cruisers was an increase in protection, particularly for the main gun turrets. The 1in non-cemented armour was replaced by 4in cemented armour on the face, with 2in non-cemented armour on the sides and roof. The extra weight required in an increase of 8in in the waterline beam to retain stability. Engine power was increased to 82,500shp, which resulted in a small increase in speed of approximately 0.3 knots.

This photograph of *Gloucester* in 1939 shows the Walrus aircraft on the catapult amidships. *Gloucester* is wearing 'neutrality stripes' on both 'B' and 'X' turrets.

This photograph of *Belfast* in August 1939 clearly displays the significant increase in distance between the superstructure and the forward funnel.

The bridge structure had a more curved profile, and included an enclosed lower bridge, which in turn led to other re-arrangements of accommodation, including the location of the captain's sea cabin. A second DCT for control of the 6in turrets was positioned on the aft superstructure, aft of the HA DCT.

EDINBURGH CLASS

The two ships of the 1936 programme, *Edinburgh* and *Belfast*, incorporated a number of significant changes, becoming much larger. Standard displacement increased to 10,550 tons and length to 613ft 6in overall. Beam also increased by a foot and the complement to 850. The armour protection was similar to that of the earlier members of the group.

The most noticeable difference in appearance was the separation of the forward funnel from the bridge structure and the siting of the mainmast before the aft funnel. The hangars were located at the aft end of the bridge structure and so the catapult was moved forward of the fore funnel, rather than being sited in between the funnels. Machinery arrangements remained similar but there was a 20% increase in bunkerage, hence extending the range. On trials, *Edinburgh* achieved a speed of 32.73 knots. (81,630shp,10,550 tons), and *Belfast* 32.98 knots. (81,140shp, 10,420 tons).

The primary gun turrets fitted were the long trunk Mk XXIII, similar to the previous Mk XXII, but with a different ammunition supply. Quadruple turrets were considered, with the guns in two pairs. Sketch designs show that the diameter of the roller path would have been maintained at 19ft but there would have been a weight increase of approximately 50 tons per mounting. 'X' and 'Y' turrets were raised one deck, and the secondary armament was increased to twelve 4in guns in six twin mountings. These were sited alongside the funnels. There was a problem with ammunition supply for these mountings, which had to

GLOUCESTER CLASS BUILDING DATA

Name	Builder	Laid down	Launched
Liverpool	Fairfield	17.02.1936	24.03.1937
Manchester	Hawthorn Leslie	28.03.1936	12.04.1937
Gloucester	Devonport Dyd	22.09.1936	19.10.1937

EDINBURGH CLASS BUILDING DATA

Name	Builder	Laid down	Launched
Belfast	Harland & Wolff	10.12.1936	17.03.1938
Edinburgh	Swan Hunter	30.12.1936	31.03.1938

A fine view of the forward turrets and bridge of *Edinburgh*, taken in 1939.

Jamaica nears completion at Vickers Armstrong's shipyard in the middle of 1942.

be transported aft on trolleys after it reached the catapult deck.

The AA armament was increased by the installation of two octuple Mk VIA*, rather than quadruple, 2pdr pom-pom mountings alongside the mainmast. The two Mk II directors were sited on the aft superstructure, forward of the HA DCT. There were also two Mk III, quadruple 0.5in machine gun mountings.

There were two DCTs for the main armament, the forward one having a 22ft rangefinder and Type 284 radar but the aft one had no radar and a 15ft rangefinder. There were three high angle directors for the 4in guns, two sided forward, one deck lower and just aft of the forward DCT, and one aft on the centreline. *Belfast* carried out trials before her 4in armament, 6in DCTs and catapult were fitted, these being installed in August/September 1939.

FIJI CLASS

The *Fiji* class were similar to the 'Town' class but more compact. Their overall

Bermuda pictured in 1942, shortly after her completion by John Brown's shipyard. Note the radar lantern in front of the bridge.

length was just 555ft 6in, partially due to the introduction of a transom stern. The beam was 4in greater than that of the *Southampton* class and 4in less than that of the *Gloucester* class. The displacement was approximately 1000 tons less, primarily due to reductions in protection. Machinery arrangements were similar but the two aft boilers were sited side-by-side rather than in tandem to reduce the overall length of the machinery, and the top speed was about 0.5 knots lower.

The primary armament was the same as that of the 'Town' class. The secondary armament of four twin 4in mountings and the AA armament of two quadruple pom-poms was also the same. Close-range weapons varied, with *Fiji*, *Kenya*, *Nigeria* and *Mauritius* receiving two quadruple 0.5in mountings, whilst *Trinidad* received four, two being sited alongside the bridge and two alongside the aft HA DCT. *Gambia* received two single pom-poms and *Bermuda*, ten single 20mm mountings. Control arrangements were also similar, but there was no after DCT for the main armament.

Aircraft arrangements were similar, apart from *Kenya* and *Fiji* which did not receive a catapult, but the complement of boats was reduced to save weight. At first glance, their appearance was very similar, but their funnels and masts were vertical, rather than raked. The first five ships were ordered under the 1937 programme, with four more authorised under the 1938 programme, and the final two ordered under the 1939 programme. When first completed, the decks of *Bermuda* were not planked.

FIJI CLASS BUILDING DATA

Name	Builder	Laid down	Launched
Nigeria	Vickers-Armstrong	08.02.1938	18.07.1939
Fiji	John Brown	30.03.1938	31.05.1939
Mauritius	Swan Hunter	31.03.1938	19.07.1939
Trinidad	Devonport Dyd	21.04.1938	21.03.1940
Kenya	Stephen	18.06.1938	18.08.1939
Jamaica	Vickers-Armstrong	28.04.1939	16.11.1940
Gambia	Swan Hunter	24.07.1939	30.11.1940
Bermuda	John Brown	30.11.1939	11.09.1941

UGANDA CLASS BUILDING DATA

Name	Builder	Laid down	Launched
Ceylon	Stephen	27.04.1939	30.07.1942
Uganda	Vickers-Armstrong	20.07.1939	07.08.1941
Newfoundland	Swan Hunter	09.11.1939	19.12.1941

UGANDA CLASS

The construction of three of the *Fiji* class was suspended, and their design was modified by reducing their primary armament to just three triple 6in turrets and increasing the AA armament with a third quadruple pom-pom mounting replacing the fourth turret. Consideration had been given to fitting a fifth twin 4in mounting but the increase in light AA armament was felt to be more important. The two original pom-pom mountings were re-sited at the forward end of the hangar deck to improve their firing arcs.

Ceylon and *Newfoundland* both completed with sixteen twin 20mm mountings, and *Uganda* completed with twenty.

Newfoundland, a year after completion displays an immaculate camouflage pattern.

Ontario (ex-*Minotaur*) displays the blue hull panel worn by many vessels later in the war.

Other features remained the same, although none of the three received planked decks.

MINOTAUR CLASS

Three more *Uganda* class cruisers were authorised under the 1941 programme – *Bellerophon*, *Swiftsure* and *Minotaur*, but *Bellerophon* was renamed *Tiger* in February 1945 and suspended in July 1946. She was not completed until March 1959 to a completely different design – see the Post War *Tiger* class. The aircraft facilities were omitted and the armament increased. An additional twin 4in mounting was fitted in place of 'X' turret, and two more quadruple pom-poms were added. The arrangement of the pom-poms was two forward, either side of the bridge and two aft, one before and one aft of the mainmast. Eight twin and six single 20mm mountings enhanced the close-range armament. Four of the twin mountings were sited either side of the fore funnel, with two more just aft of them, on the main deck. The final two were fitted aft of the mainmast, on the same level as the pom-poms. The single mountings were fitted either side of the main DCT, one deck below, on the boat deck, either side of the crane, and either side of the mainmast. The beam was increased to 63ft to maintain stability.

Superb was authorised under the 1941 supplementary programme, and underwent further modifications while under construction, which resulted in a further increase in beam to 64ft, and additional armament of two single pom-poms and eight single 40mm Bofors mountings, the number of 20mm mountings being reduced to two single and two twin. This is sometimes referred to as the 'revised' *Tiger* design.

Superb in autumn 1946.

MINOTAUR CLASS BUILDING DATA

Name	Builder	Laid down	Launched
*Minotaur**	Harland & Wolff	20.11.1941	29.7.1943
Swiftsure	Vickers-Armstrong	22.9.1941	4.2.1943
Superb	Swan Hunter	23.6.1942	31.8.1943

* Transferred to RCN as HMCS *Ontario* on completion.

Wartime Modifications

SOUTHAMPTON CLASS

SOUTHAMPTON – Radar Type 279 was fitted in May 1940 while the ship was at Rosyth, but she was lost in January 1941 before any other modifications could be carried out.

SHEFFIELD – The first radar Type 79Y was fitted in 1938. Radar Types 284 and 285 were fitted in the summer of 1941 at Rosyth, and six single 20mm Oerlikons were added and the 0.5in MGs landed in September. The 20mm were located one on each of 'B' and 'X' turret, two on the lower bridge and two on the aft control platform. Whilst on the Tyne in April–July 1942, radar Type 279 was replaced by Types 281, 282, 283 and 273, and three more 20mm singles were added. That on 'B' turret was removed but two were added on each of the lower bridge and aft control platforms.

On the Clyde during March–June 1943, five more 20mm singles were added. Aircraft facilities were removed during January–February 1944 whilst at Liverpool,

Sheffield on convoy escort duty, with small calibre AA guns on 'X' turret, before its removal. The AA guns on 'B' turret have been removed.

Sheffield in June 1946, after the removal of the aircraft facilities and 'X' turret.

Newcastle in New York in November 1942, wearing the Admiralty scheme of B5, 507c and B15.

and eight single 20mm added. *Sheffield* underwent a major refit in Boston, USA from July 1944 to May 1945, when 'X' turret, fifteen 20mm guns and radar Type 273 were removed. Four quadruple 40mm and ten twin power operated 20mm were added, with radar Type 277. Single 40mm Bofors had replaced the twin 20mm Oerlikons by 1946.

NEWCASTLE – Two UP [unrotated projectile] mountings were fitted in April–May 1940, whilst on the Tyne. In April–May 1941, at Simonstown, radar Type 286 was fitted. Whilst undergoing a refit during September–November 1941 at Boston, USA, the UP mountings, 0.5in MGs and radar Type 286 were removed, but *Newcastle* received radars Type 273 and 291, and nine single 20mm Oerlikons – one on 'B' turret, two on the lower bridge and four on the aft control platform. In New York during October–November 1942 the aircraft facilities were removed, as was radar Type 291. Ten single 20mm Oerlikons and radars Type 281, 284 and 285 were fitted. In July–September 1943, at Simonstown, six single mountings were replaced by four twin 20mm guns. During May–October 1945, a major refit included the removal of 'X' turret.

BIRMINGHAM – A UP mounting was added in June 1940 at Rosyth, but landed in July 1941 at Simonstown. In Simonstown again in March 1942, the 0.5in MGs were removed, and seven single 20mm Oerlikons and radars Type 284 and 291 added. At Devonport, between April and August 1943, the aircraft facilities, five single 20mm Oerlikons and radar Type 291 were removed. Eight twin 20mm Oerlikons (one each on 'B' and 'X' turrets, two on the lower bridge and four on the catapult deck) were added, as were radar Type 281 and 273. 'X' turret was removed, and four 40mm quadruple Bofors, two twin and five single 20mm Oerlikons added between July and November 1944, during a refit at Norfolk, Virginia. She was 'fitted-for-but-not-with' radar Type 293 at the top of the foremast before February 1945.

GLASGOW – Two UP mountings and radar Type 286 were added in summer 1940 at Liverpool. The UP mountings were removed a year later in Singapore. At New York, during the summer of 1942, the 0.5in MGs and radar Type 279 were removed, radar Types 273, 281, 282, 284 and 285 were fitted, together with nine single 20mm Oerlikons. On the Clyde in December 1942, five single Oerlikons were removed and eight twin 20mm added. At Devonport, during autumn 1943, two more single 20mm Oerlikons were added. Whilst undergoing a refit at Portsmouth from June 1944 to May 1945, 'X' turret, two twin and four single 20mm Oerlikons, the aircraft facilities and radars Type 273, 281 and 284 were all landed, and two quadruple and four single pom-poms added, together with radars Type 281, 274 and 293. She was also fitted with an aircraft homing beacon Type YE.

Birmingham at Norfolk Navy Yard on 16 November 1944. Note the zareba on top of 'B' turret, the carley floats on the sides of both 'A' and 'B' turrets and the blue hull panel.

GLOUCESTER CLASS

LIVERPOOL – In October 1940 *Liverpool* was hit by an aircraft torpedo and whilst at Alexandria, undergoing emergency repairs, in October 1940–April 1941 two quadruple 2pdr pom-poms and two quad 0.5in MGs were removed. Permanent repairs were carried out at Mare Island, California from June to November 1941, when nine single 20mm Oerlikons were added, one each on 'B' and 'X' turrets, one on the quarterdeck, two on the lower bridge and four on the aft control platform. The quad 2pdr pom-poms were restored on her return to the Clyde, December 1941–January 1942. Radar Types 284, 285, 282 and 273 were also fitted. Whilst at Lyness in February 1942, radar Type 281 was added. *Liverpool* underwent a refit at Rosyth from August 1942 to July 1945, when the aircraft facilities, two 20mm Oerlikons, radar Types 281, 273 and 284, and 'X' gun were all removed. Four (or six) quad and four single 2pdr pom-poms were added. It is also reported that either seven 40mm single Bofors and five single 20mm Oerlikons, or six twin 20mm Oerlikons were added – unable to confirm which. Radars Type 279, 293, 277, 274 and 283 were also fitted.

Glasgow leaving New York Navy Yard in August 1942.

Liverpool at Mare Island in October 1941, following her repair.

MANCHESTER – At Rosyth in November 1940 radar Type 286 was fitted. Whilst on the Tyne, January–March 1941, the 0.5in MGs were removed, and a Bofors Mk III on 'B' turret and five 20mm Oerlikons were added. *Manchester* was under refit in Philadelphia, USA, from September 1941 to February 1942, when the radar Type 286 was removed and replaced by Types 273, 279, 282, 284 and 285. Eight single 20mm Oerlikons were fitted, located two on lower bridge, four on aft control platform, one on 'X' turret and one on the quarterdeck. Three 40mm single Bofors (Army type?) and five 20mm Oerlikons had been added by the time of her loss in August 1942.

GLOUCESTER – Not modified before her loss in May 1941.

EDINBURGH CLASS

BELFAST – *Belfast* was badly damaged by a magnetic mine in November 1939, which broke her back. She underwent temporary repairs at Rosyth until June 1940, before moving to Devonport for permanent repairs, which lasted until December 1942. During this period, she received a bulge, increasing her beam by approximately three feet.

During the repairs, the quadruple 0.5in mountings were removed, and four single 20mm Oerlikons on Mk IV mountings were sited adjacent to the catapult, and five twin Mk VB mountings were fitted, two on the quarterdeck, two on the hangar roof and one on 'B' turret during her refit. Radars Type 281, 282, 283, 284 and 285 were added and a Type 273 lantern was fitted aft of the forward DCT.

In June 1943, during a docking at Rosyth, four more single 20mm guns were added. The sheet anchor was removed and the hawse pipe plated over. *Belfast* returned to Rosyth in April–May 1944 for another docking and during this time six more 20mm guns were added and a twin mounting was removed.

During a refit on the Tyne, between August 1944 and May 1945, to improve the accommodation for operations in the Pacific, two of the 4in twin mountings, the aircraft facilities and eight single 20mm mountings were removed. Four quadruple and four single pom-poms were added. Radar Types 281b, 293, 277, 274 and 268 replaced Types 281, 284 and 273.

Belfast underwent another docking in August 1945, this time in Sydney, Australia, when two twin 20mm mountings were removed, and three single Bofors Mk III,

Belfast in 1942, after repair.

A close view of the aft port side of *Edinburgh* in 1942.

and two 'Boffins' (twin Oerlikon 20mm Mk V mountings converted to accommodate a single Bofors 40mm gun) were fitted.

EDINBURGH – *Edinburgh* underwent a refit at South Shields from March to October 1940, when radar Type 279 was fitted. Six single 20mm Oerlikon guns were added when she was at Gibraltar during July 1941, two on 'B' turret, two on the forward superstructure and two on the quarterdeck. During her refit on the Tyne from January to March 1942, radar Types 284, 285 and 273 were fitted.

FIJI CLASS

NIGERIA – Four single 20mm Oerlikons had been added before she was involved in a collision in September 1941. During repairs on the Tyne, lasting until the end of the year, radar Types 273 and 284 were fitted. After being torpedoed in August 1942, *Nigeria* went to Charlestown, USA, for repairs, which lasted until June 1943. During this time, the 0.5in MGs and single 20mm mounts were removed, as was the port aircraft crane. Radar Type 273 was replaced by Types 272 and 282, and eight twin 20mm mountings were fitted.

On her return to Great Britain, the remainder of the aircraft arrangements were removed in the winter of 1943, and radar Type 283 was fitted. By the end of the war, *Nigeria* had received three single 40mm Bofors Mk III mountings.

FIJI – *Fiji* was torpedoed in September 1940, and underwent six months of repairs, during which two additional quadruple 0.5in MGs and radar Type 284 were fitted. There were no other changes before she was sunk in May 1941.

MAURITIUS – Whilst under refit on the Tyne in early 1942, *Mauritius* had her AA armament enhanced by the addition of four single 20mm Oerlikon guns and received radar Types 284, 285 and 273. During a passage through the Suez Canal in June 1943, the aircraft facilities were removed and twenty additional 20mm guns added.

After grounding in June 1943, she was under repair at Alexandria, when her two quad 0.5in MGs were removed. She received another refit at Chatham in April–May 1944, when the port aircraft crane was removed and a Type 650 missile jamming system was added. 'X' turret was removed during 1945.

TRINIDAD – details of *Trinidad*'s modifications are unknown, but by May 1942, when she was sunk, two single 20mm guns had been fitted on the quarterdeck.

Nigeria in June 1943, following her refit in Charlestown, USA.

Kenya has had her 'X' turret removed and replaced by twin 40mm guns.

KENYA – Following a collision, *Kenya* was repaired at Rosyth (July–August 1941) when two quadruple 0.5in MGs and two single 20mm guns were added. She docked at Rosyth in December 1941, when radar Types 284 and 273 were fitted. After being torpedoed in 1942, repairs were carried out on the Tyne, when the four quadruple 0.5in MGs and two single 20mm guns were removed, to be replaced by six twin 20mm mountings. Radar Types 285, 283, 282 and 272 were fitted, replacing the Type 273.

By late 1943, two additional twin 20mm mountings had been fitted, and during a refit at Durban in April 1945, 'X' turret was removed and replaced by two twin 40mm Bofors mountings. At the end of the war, the pom-poms were removed and replaced by twin 40mm mountings, and the twin 20mm mountings were replaced by single 40mm mountings.

JAMAICA – The AA armament was increased to five quadruple and four single pom-poms. Eight twin 20mm mountings were added during 1943. Two single Bofors were added later. The aircraft arrangements and 'X' turret were removed during a refit in 1944–45, and the two aircraft cranes were replaced with one on the centreline.

Bermuda in December 1945 following the removal of 'X' turret and the fitting of pom-pom mountings.

Uganda in October 1944 at the end of her US refit. The port crane and aircraft facilities have been removed, and US quad 40mm Bofors mounts sited, port and starboard, on the old catapult deck. Note the carley floats on the side of the forward superstructure.

A stump mast was fitted forward of the aft funnel to carry a YE aircraft homing beacon.

GAMBIA – Six single 20mm guns were added whilst completing in February 1942. *Gambia* was at Liverpool from June to September 1943, during which time the aircraft arrangements, two single pom-poms, and six single 20mm guns were removed, and ten twin 20mm mountings added, six on the aft superstructure, two amidships where the aircraft catapult had been located, and two forward, adjacent to the HA DCTs. Some sources show two single 20mm guns retained on platforms on the forward face of the bridge and two on platforms just aft of the mainmast. Radar Types 272 and 283 replaced Type 273.

BERMUDA – During a docking at Devonport in September 1943, six single 20mm guns were added. She had a refit on the Tyne in April–May 1944, when her aircraft arrangements and twelve single 20mm guns were removed, to be replaced by eight twin 20mm mountings.

Bermuda underwent a major refit at Glasgow, from June 1944 to April 1945, when 'X' turret and four twin 20mm mount-

Newfoundland in 1944, following her refit on the Clyde.

This starboard side view of *Swiftsure*, taken in August 1946, clearly shows the two 40mm guns sited alongside the forward funnel, and the single and twin mountings aft of the after funnel.

ings were removed. Three quadruple and four single pom-poms were fitted in their place. Radar Types 281 and 272 were replaced by Types 293, 277 and 281b. During a refit in Sydney, Australia, in August 1945, two twin and two single 20mm mountings were removed, and replaced by two single Bofors Mk III and two 'Boffin' mountings.

UGANDA CLASS

CEYLON – By April 1944, *Ceylon* had had two twin and eight single 20mm mountings added. During the summer, she received another two twin and eight single 20mm mountings. The four twin and six of the single mountings had been removed and replaced by four single Bofors Mk III mountings by September the following year.

This view of the aft superstructure of *Superb* in 1946 highlights the collection of AA guns located there.

UGANDA – Following damage by a guided missile at Salerno Bay in September 1943, *Uganda* was under repair for twelve months at Charlestown, USA, followed by further work in a British yard until June 1945. During this time, the port crane and the aircraft facilities were removed and radar Type 283 added; the existing three quad pom-poms were augmented by two US quad 40mm Bofors, and the rest of the light AA fit comprised four twin 20mm Mk V mountings and eight single 20mm mountings. Radar Types 281b, 274, 277 and 293 later replaced Types 281, 284, 272 and 283.

NEWFOUNDLAND – *Newfoundland* received temporary repairs at Malta during July–August 1943, after being torpedoed. She then went to Boston, USA, until April 1944, for permanent repairs. On her return to Great Britain, she went to the Clyde, for a refit, which lasted until November 1944. During this period, her aircraft arrangements were removed, and two quadruple Bofors, and two twin and two single 20mm mountings were fitted. Radar Types 281b, 274, 277 and 293 replaced Types 281, 274 and 272.

MINOTAUR CLASS

Minotaur – As HMCS *Ontario*, she received additional insulation and steam heating, and carried six single 40mm and six single 20mm mountings at the end of the war. This was later changed to three quadruple and three single 40mm mountings.

Swiftsure – *Swiftsure* underwent a refit in Sydney, Australia, in June–August 1945 when eight twin and six single 20mm gun mountings were removed and replaced by eight Boffins and five single Bofors Mk III mountings.

Superb – At the end of the war, *Superb* had four quadruple 2pdr pom-pom and eight 40mm Bofors guns.

Model Products

NAVIS-NEPTUN

1:1250 scale

Navis-Neptun of Germany produce the largest range of 1:1250 scale metal models, including ships from many countries, and of many eras. The range is so large that not all models can be in production at any one time, frequently resulting in long waiting times when a modeller requires a specific model.

The range includes: 1140 *Nigeria*; 1140a *Uganda*; 11430b *Swiftsure* (not listed 2022); 1142 *Belfast*; 1142a *Edinburgh*; 1143 *Manchester*; 1143a *Sheffield*; 1143b *Birmingham* (not listed 2022).

They are normally painted grey overall, with highlights such as black funnel tops and brown tops to boats. The details are fine, and the models are generally accurate. Pictured are (left to right) – limited edition of *Sheffield* in camouflage, *Sheffield*, *Birmingham* and *Belfast*.

JOHN'S MODEL SHIPYARD

1:1200 scale

The small British company, John's Model Shipyard, produce a series of 3D print resin kits, including the 'Town' class cruiser, with a square bridge (RN305). The kit moulds the hull, superstructure and tripod masts as a single piece, with separate turrets. Six turrets are supplied, three with AA armament on top. *Sheffield*, *Newcastle*, *Southampton* and *Glasgow* can be completed from this kit – *Birmingham* had no knuckle on the hull at the bow and the Batch 2 'Town' class had rounded bridge fronts.

Kits of *Leander* as in 1939 (RN322) and as in 1942 (RN327) have become available since ShipCraft 31 was published.

SKYTREX

1:700 scale

The British company Skytrex produce a number of metal warship models – 1:350 scale World War II Royal Navy warships and 1:700 scale modern 'fast attack craft' from a variety of different navies. Their 1:700 scale World War II Royal Navy warships are no longer listed.

The models of *Swiftsure* (MD17) and *Kenya* (MD13) are finely cast, with the exception of the masts, which are oversize. The models are painted dark grey and light grey (respectively) overall, with a black funnel tops and anchor chains. The gun barrels of the small AA mounts are also painted black on *Kenya* but remain grey on *Swiftsure*, and the carley floats ochre. No aircraft is included with the model of *Kenya*.

MT MINIATURES 1:700 scale

HMS *Tiger* (MTM031) is a one-piece resin moulding of a waterline hull and the majority of the superstructure. Details, such as gun turrets, are supplied in white metal, poorly cast. Surprisingly, the forward face of the superstructure is supplied in white metal and is not part of the resin moulding. An etched brass sheet

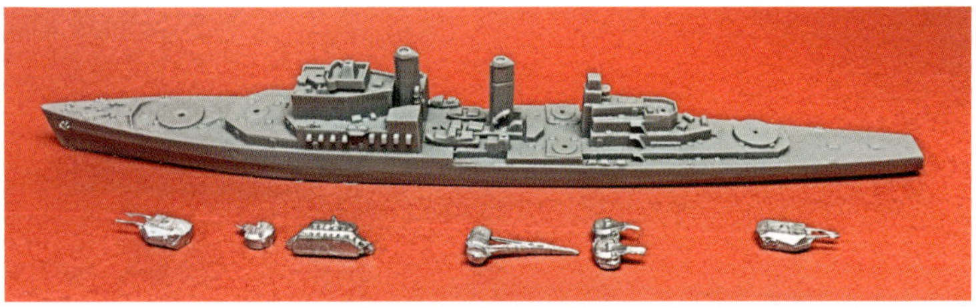

provides a very limited quantity of guard-wires, the lattice masts and yards. There are no decals.

Instructions comprise just a single assembly drawing, and no colour details are provided.

B-RESINA 1:700 scale

This resin kit from Czechia depicts *Belfast* as in December 1943, during the Battle of North Cape. Inspiration for this model came from the Airfix 1:600 scale version, and so it includes some of the same errors, but it has been accurately scaled to the smaller size.

The moulding is clean, although the bulwarks on the hull moulding are thick, and detailed parts do have some flash on them. The use of etched brass will bring great improvements for the crane jib,

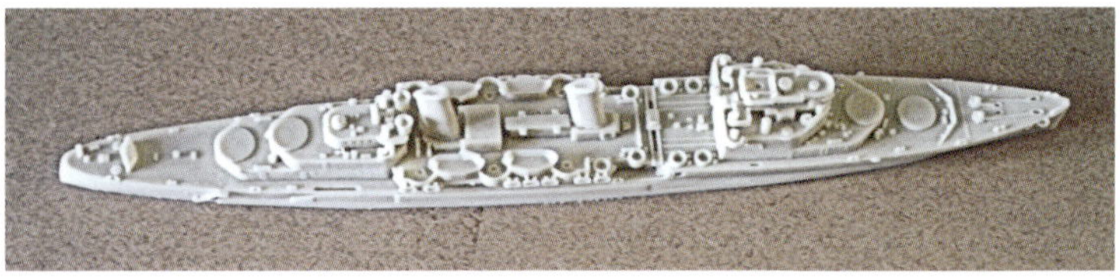

various radar aerials and other fine details. The masts are best made from wire, using the dimensions of the resin parts.

Etched brass details will also enhance the Walrus aircraft, but as it was removed in June 1943, it could be omitted. Different sources provide varying details for the number and types of boats carried, and their locations, so it is worth checking elsewhere rather than depending on the instructions. The instructions come on just a single, double-sided piece of A4 paper,

containing one assembly drawing and a colour scheme. The colours given have generic names, *eg* 'pale blue-grey', and it is worth consulting other sources for more precise details regarding both colour and pattern.

The primary gun turrets are good representations, but this is not the same for the secondary and AA guns. These should be replaced with after-market parts if possible.

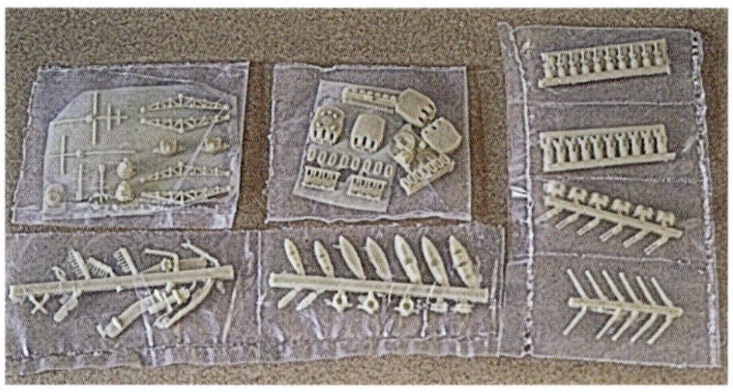

MATCHBOX 1:700 SCALE

HMS *Tiger* was first released in 1979, but was re-released in 1986 and again in 1992, with the new box-top artwork shown. Revell released the kit in 2012.

It is a waterline kit moulded on three sprues, the one for the hull being a dark grey and the two for the deck and superstructure being much lighter in colour. The kit represents the cruiser after modification to a helicopter carrier.

The mouldings, in particular the sprues, are rather thick and lack detail. This is particularly noticeable on the mouldings for the lattice mast and the Type 965 radar

antenna, both of which need replacing with photo-etch parts. The decals include hull numbers, flight deck markings and a white ensign.

This kit is a good basis for super-detailing with after-market parts.

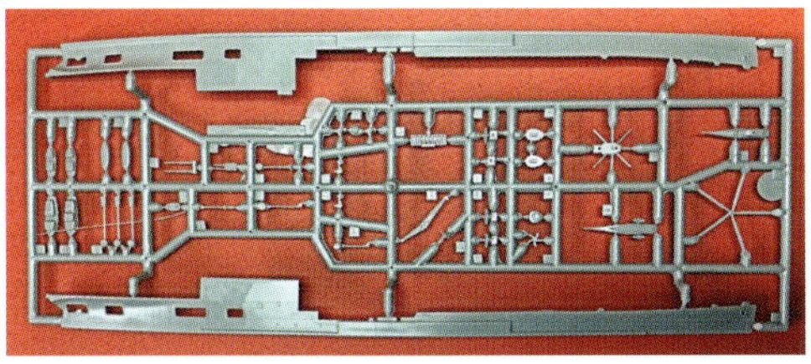

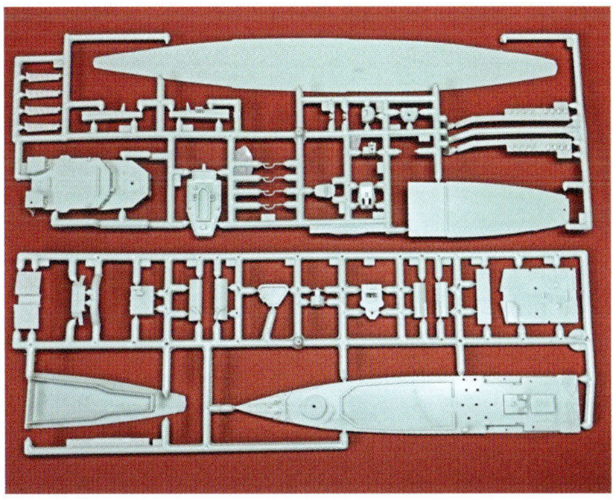

WHITE ENSIGN MODELS

1:700 & 1:350 scale

Before ceasing trading in the UK and the sale to Tom's Modelworks in the USA, White Ensign Models released two resin kits at 1:700 scale and one at 1:350 scale of the 'Town' class cruisers *Sheffield* and *Edinburgh*. Subsequently one of these, *Edinburgh*, was released by Atlantic Models.

In the sample of HMS *Sheffield* 1941 (WEM K 706), the hull was warped and required flattening before use, but it was cleanly cast, apart from the waterline which requires a significant amount of cleaning up. The major parts of the superstructure are moulded integrally with the hull, the hangar area being hollow. The other super-structure parts are in one plastic bag, and care is needed when making the cut-out in the flying deck aft of the funnels to ensure a good fit over the superstructure. The other resin parts are supplied in two more bags, all needing a small amount of cleaning up.

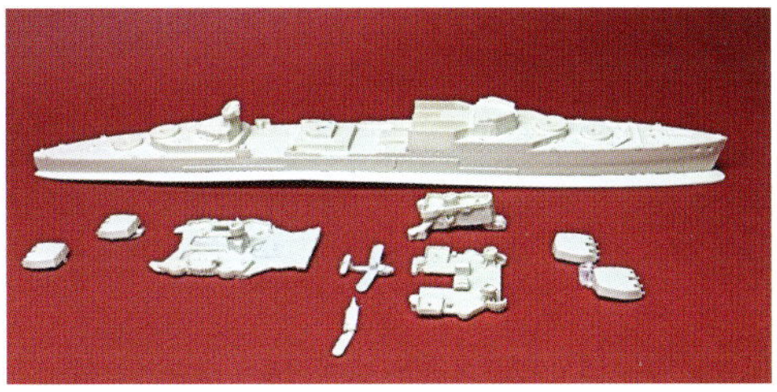

The masters for the extensive etched brass were produced by Peter Hall (the proprietor of Atlantic Models), and so the same sheet as that for *Edinburgh* is also included in this kit. The instruction are extensive, clear and simple to follow and the colour scheme is given for the cruiser in May 1941.

WEM once produced a superb 1:350 scale model of *Sheffield*, but it suffered from difficulties in casting, and has not been re-released.

(Photograph courtesy of Ian Ruscoe)

ATLANTIC MODELS

1:700 scale

The waterline hull of HMS *Edinburgh* as in 1941 (ATK 70024) has areas of superstructure moulded integrally. The forward superstructure is hollow to allow the representation of the hangars and is completed by affixing the rear face and deck, which fit almost perfectly. The hangar doors are moulded closed and will need to be removed if the modeller wishes to show the aircraft stowed. The bridge moulding fits on the deck, and a deck is supplied

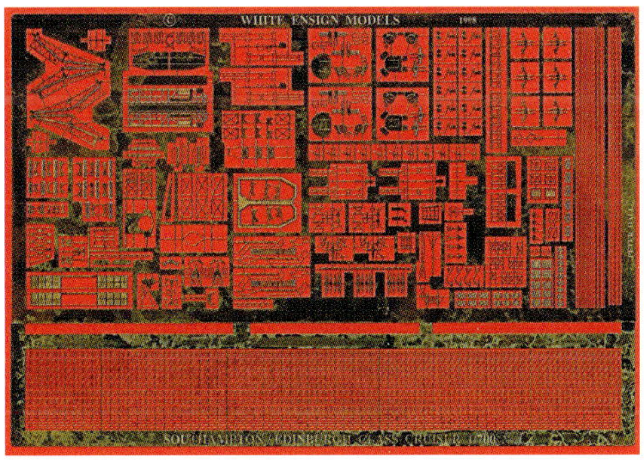

which fits over the two midships superstructure blocks, to which the funnels and other details are added. Resin barrels for the primary guns are provided separately, and some may prefer to replace them with turned brass parts. Two aircraft are included with their wings deployed, and so will need cutting if they are to be stowed.

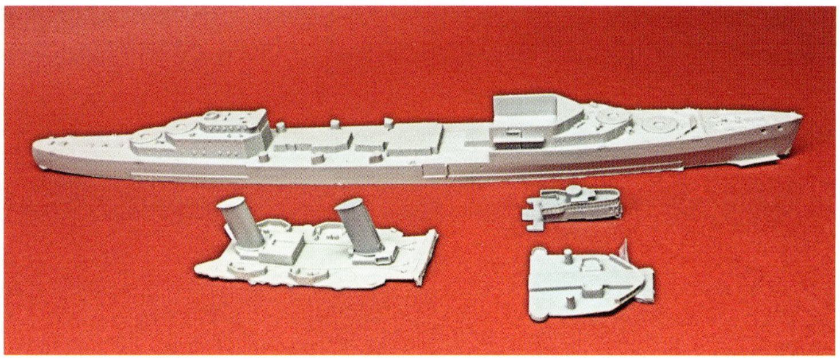

There is an extensive photo-etch sheet, but not all parts are used on this single model. The guardwires are generic and so will need to be cut to length. Instructions are provided on six double-sided A4 sheets and include a painting diagram for the cruiser as in 1939 – not 1941 as indicated on the box.

L'ARSENAL 1:700 scale

HMS *Jamaica* 1942 (700-17) is the only small-scale kit of a 'Colony' class cruiser available, and was first released in a compact package containing a waterline resin hull, and nine bags of resin components. The hull was slightly warped, but this could easily be corrected with some warm water and weights. The 'pours' are substantial, and care will be required when removing the parts, particularly the smaller ones, of which there are many. Many of the components do have flash that needs to be removed. The forward superstructure is partially hollow to represent the hangars. All parts are highly detailed.

There is also an extensive photo-etch sheet, and turned brass gun barrels and masts from Master-Model of Poland. Instructions are provided on nine double-sided A4 sheets, depicting the construction in 29 steps. Camouflage details are also given, the colours being identified by Admiralty numbers.

Re-released in 2022 in the same box, the parts are now produced using 3D printing techniques. Due to limitations on the size of printed parts, the hull is in two sections. These parts are hollow and need to be cut to length, and then joined, an internal part being included to ensure correct alignment.

Construction is very similar, with the photo-etch sheet being identical. The boats are resin castings, as supplied in the previous release. The colour details supplied are identical.

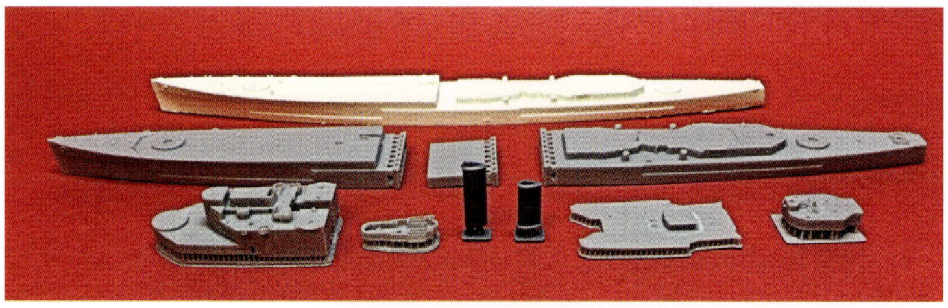

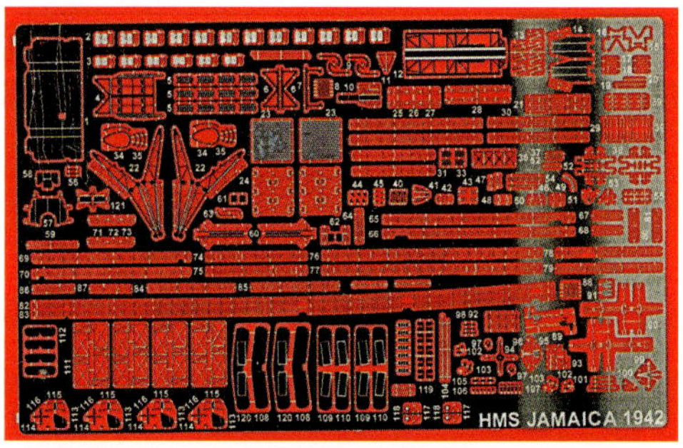

This model of HMS *Sheffield* 1942 (700-16) is similar to that of *Jamaica*, and, with few changes, the same comments apply. With the 3D printed later model, the hull is divided into three parts.

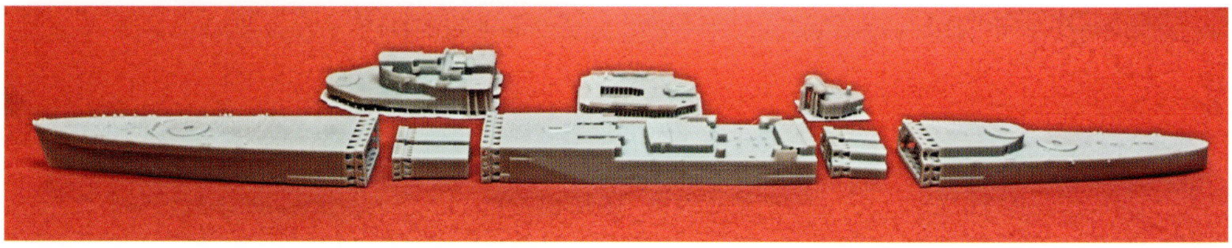

TRUMPETER

1:700 & 1:350 scales

Trumpeter have released two models of *Belfast*, as in 1942 – a 1:700 scale waterline model and a 1:350 scale full-hull model. The smaller model was released in 2022, and employs the latest tooling techniques, resulting in some significant differences to the larger model that was released a few years earlier.

The waterline hull is a single-piece moulding, including the base, with two deck pieces. There are five separate main superstructure mouldings, with the smaller mouldings and midships deck on one of the sprues. There are five different sprues, two of which are duplicated. Two aircraft are supplied on a clear sprue, to enable realistic painting of the cockpit. There is a small photo-etch sheet, containing the two cranes, platform supports, funnel grilles and radar antennas, but no guardwires. The decal sheet includes roundels for the aircraft. Instructions are provided in sixteen assembly diagrams. The colour instructions are not the same as those supplied with the larger model, the main differences being in the areas of wooden deck.

The hull of the larger model is split along the centreline, the two halves being joined by seven bulkheads to ensure accurate alignment and adequate stiffness. There are seven different sprues, one of

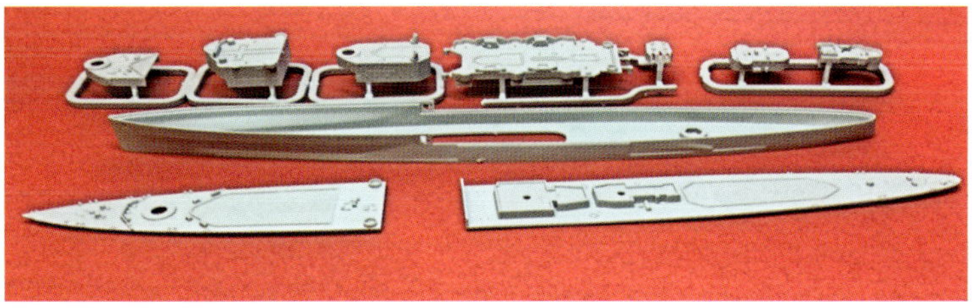

which is duplicated, and including four copies of the sprue containing the 6in gun turrets. There are two aircraft sprues, moulded in clear plastic, and one sprue containing the stand for the model. There is a photo-etched sheet containing ladders, funnel grilles and radar antennas, but the cranes are moulded in plastic and there are no guardwires. There is a short length of brass anchor chain, and the instructions are provided in twenty-eight assembly diagrams. One error is that the funnels are 'too fat' – see Accessories.

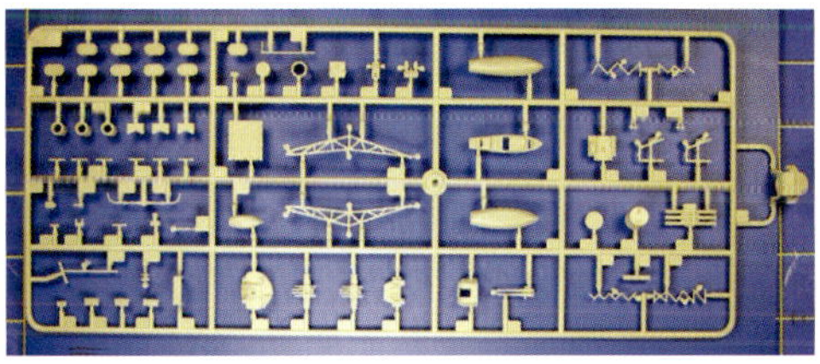

In 2023, Trumpeter also released a second model in 1:700 scale, representing *Belfast* as in 1959. This is similar to their other kit of her in 1942, the most obvious difference being the inclusion of a sheet of etched brass containing the two lattice masts.

Note: Trumpeter do produce a photo-etch sheet of 1/700 Handrails & Ladders, 06634.

AIRFIX

1:600 scale

Airfix first released their model of *Belfast* in 1973, and it has been re-released a number of times, although without retooling. It takes the normal form of a full hull, split along the centreline, with the deck being provided in two pieces. There is an indentation on the inside of each half of the hull indicating the waterline, which will be a great help to many. There are four sprues of components. Items, such as masts and davits, are much finer than in the earlier kits, but items, such as boats, still lack detail.

The large superstructures are provided with two separate sides and deck, which does allow some detail to be moulded onto the outsides of the superstructure. The fit is generally good, and there is no flash – at

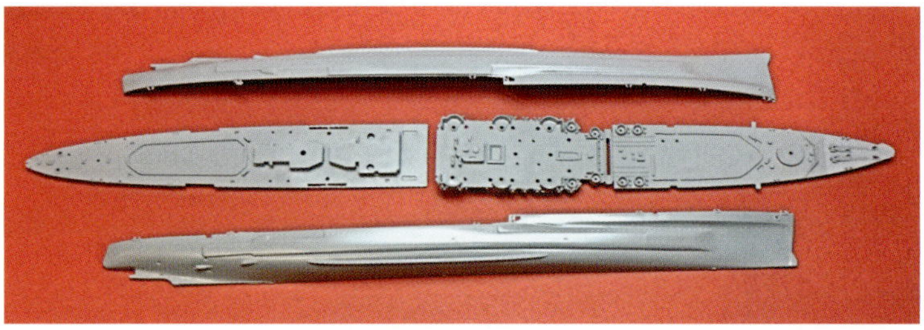

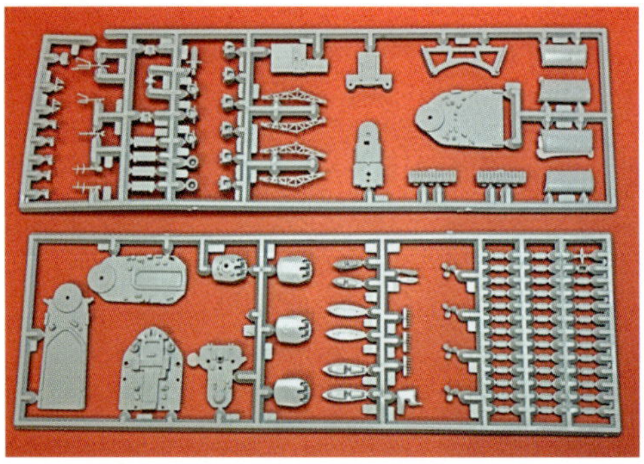

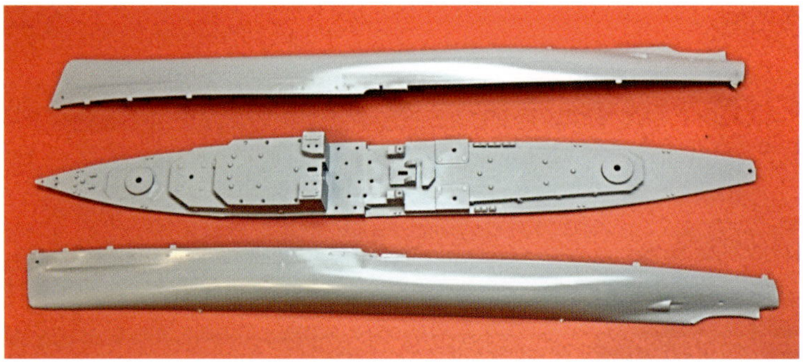

least not on the early releases, although this has increased on some re-releases as the tooling wears.

Instructions are provided on a large sheet, each side of which has three pages. There are seventeen assembly diagrams, plus a detailed camouflage scheme, and a introduction to the vessel – in three languages. This kit provides a good basis, which, with some after-market detail parts, will produce a fine accurate model.

HMS *Tiger* was the third twentieth-century warship to be released by Airfix, in 1960. It was re-released in 1967 and 1973, each time with new box-top artwork; that from 1973 is shown. It represents the cruiser 'as built', and suffers from the common limitations of moulding ability of the time – items such as lattice masts are thick and there is little detail on the superstructure, gun mountings, boats and other fittings. However, there is only a minimal amount of flash.

The full hull is moulded in two halves, but there is no waterline on the inside as for *Belfast*. The deck is a single-piece moulding, with bollards and liferafts moulded integrally. Once again this is a good basic model but needs a lot of detailing to bring it up to current standards.

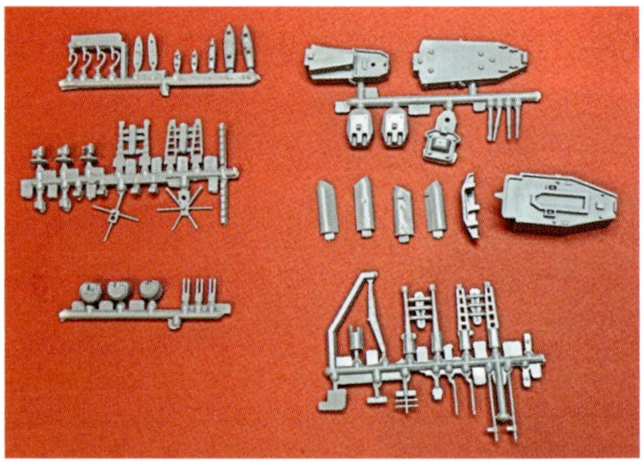

FROG 1:415 scale

This kit of HMS *Tiger* (F.142) was originally released in 1961 and re-issued in 1970 with the box artwork shown. It has since been issued by Novo and Eastern Express, being referred to as a 'battleship' by the last of these manufacturers. The latest release, in 2012, was by Ark Models.

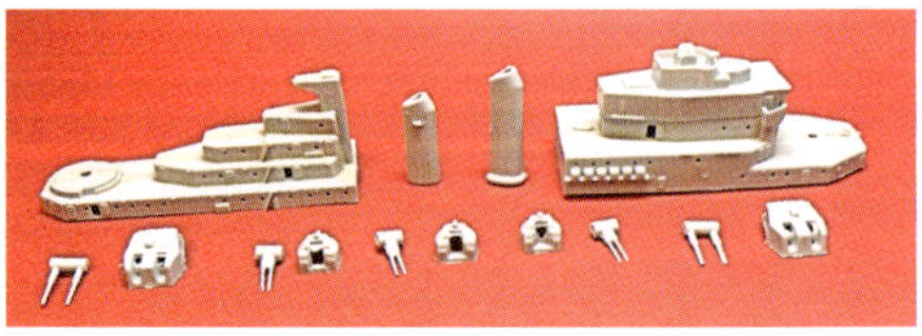

It is a full hull model, split along the centreline. The mouldings are substantial and basically accurate, but devoid of detail. One unusual feature is the provision of decals for the lattice mast. These are printed in black and wrap round the solid masts. Decals are also included for the bridge windows and draft marks. Instructions are basic, comprising fourteen assembly diagrams.

This kit needs a great deal of modification to produce a worthwhile model.

JSC

1:400 scale

This card model from Poland of HMS *Sheffield* is supplied in an A4 size book containing two sheets of instructions and six sheets of card. The instructions are provided in both Polish and English. Inside the front cover are some black and white photographs of a completed model, and inside the back cover is a general arrangement drawing showing the location of the parts. The card sheets include both coloured parts and black and white constructional parts for the hull. The coloured parts are well printed and clearly identified. Lattice parts, such as the crane jibs, are printed grey with black spaces in between. Some modellers may consider cutting out the black areas or replacing the items with etched brass, for enhanced realism. The components for the masts are illustrated full size, but the diameters of the brass wire are not given. The parts for the Walrus aircraft are included on the back cover.

IRON SHIPWRIGHTS

1:350 scale

This American model of HMS *Sheffield* (4-038) is a full-hull, resin moulding, with the hull incorporating the main parts of the superstructure, including the bridge. The hull is cleanly moulded, with cleaning up being required along the centreline, on the bottom of the hull. The plating, especially the armour belt is rather pronounced. The main parts of the superstructure and primary gun turrets are also cleanly moulded, requiring only a little cleaning up, but the smaller details have a lot of flash to be removed before they can be used.

There is also an extensive etched brass sheet, and brass rod, of various diameters, for the masts, although resin masts are also included. Instructions are provided in a pictorial format. The model represents *Sheffield* as in 1941, but details need to be checked to ensure an accurate model. No colour details are included.

This kit provides a good basis for an accurate model, although replacement of the details by after-market parts will greatly enhance the result.

MODELIK

1:200 scale

This large card model of HMS *Sheffield*, again from Poland, is supplied in an A3

size book containing five sheets of paper and eight sheets of printed colour card. Inside the front cover is an introduction to the ship, in Polish. The five sheets of paper contain a general arrangement drawing, showing the location of parts, assembly drawings of the smaller parts, including the masts, and structural parts, such as the bulkheads and keel. The latter will need to be affixed to thicker card before use. The coloured parts are well printed and clearly identified, with the location of adjacent parts indicated.

FLEETSCALE

1:128 scale

For those wishing to build a working model, Fleetscale, of the United Kingdom, produce a GRP hull, with plate, rivet, armour and porthole detail. They can also provide a general arrangement drawing of *Gambia* (this does not contain instructions or construction information), a four-shaft running gear set, glazed ports, both bow jackstaff and stern ensign staff, an etched brass crane, and two sets of details

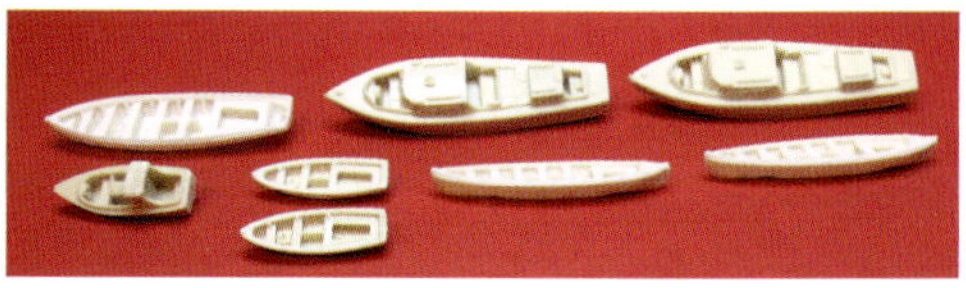

produced by Quaycraft, a set of eight boats and a set of general fittings, including both gun and torpedo armament, fairleads and bollards, hatches and doors, paravanes, carley rafts, anchors, funnel caps and davits.

The modeller must scratch-build the superstructure, but many of the more difficult details are included in the set.

ACCESSORIES

MICROMASTER

Various scales

MicroMaster began selling their 3D printed products via the Shapeways website, but now have their own production facilities in New Zealand. Many of their products are still available from Shapeways, but since starting their own production, MicroMaster have significantly increased their range, and the new items are only available direct. The Shapeways items are produced in a translucent material, but those from MicroMaster are in a grey plastic. Not only do they produce items in the popular scales for small scale models

(*ie* 1:700, 1:600 & 1:350), but some are also available at larger scales, such as 1:96 and 1:72, used for working models.

Particular items of interest include a number of 1:600 scale parts for use with the various Airfix kits of *Belfast* and *Tiger*. The most useful are the gun turrets which include the triple 6in turrets (a similar set is also available for the 'Colony' class cruisers), and the twin 4in turrets, and for the *Tiger* there are the twin 6in and twin 3in turrets. Common items such as torpedo tubes, rangefinders, searchlights, boats and carley floats are also available.

They are all highly detailed and will enhance the original kit.

BOGEYS BITS

1:415, 1:600, 1:700 scales

The British company, Bogeys Bits, also sell their 3D printed products via the Shapeways website. The Shapeways items are produced in a translucent material, and Bogeys Bits produce items in a number of popular scales for smaller models.

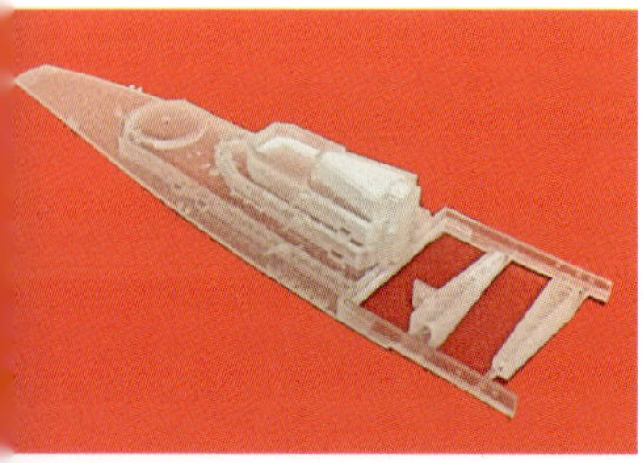

Particular items of interest are for the various scale kits of *Tiger*. These include a set for the Matchbox/Revell command cruiser at 1:700 scale, the Airfix cruiser at 1:600 scale and the Frog/Novo cruiser at 1:415 scale. Bogeys Bits also produce the aft superstructure of the original cruiser and a detail set at 1:700 scale to enable the Matchbox/Revell kit to be returned to the cruiser's original configuration.

The detail sets are similar, and include a range of replacement parts, including gun

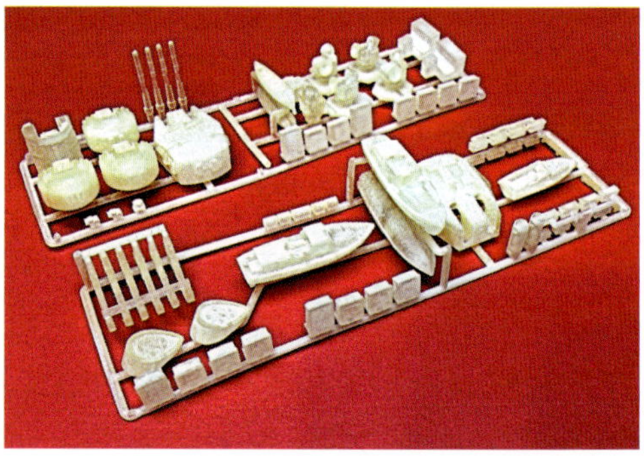

turrets and boats, and some additional parts such as a Land Rover vehicle. The conversion of the command cruiser back to the original configuration will also require a significant amount of scratch-building.

BILL'S MODELS

1:600 scale

Bill's Models, from the USA, sell their 3D printed products via the Shapeways website also. The Shapeways items are produced in a translucent material, and Bill's Models produce items in a number of popular scales for small scale models.

A particular item of interest is the flight-deck to assist with the modification of the Airfix kit of *Tiger* to represent her as modified to a helicopter carrier. The transition from the original hull to the overhanging flightdeck is, probably, the most difficult part of the modification, and this part also includes a basic hangar, 'flyco' office and mast.

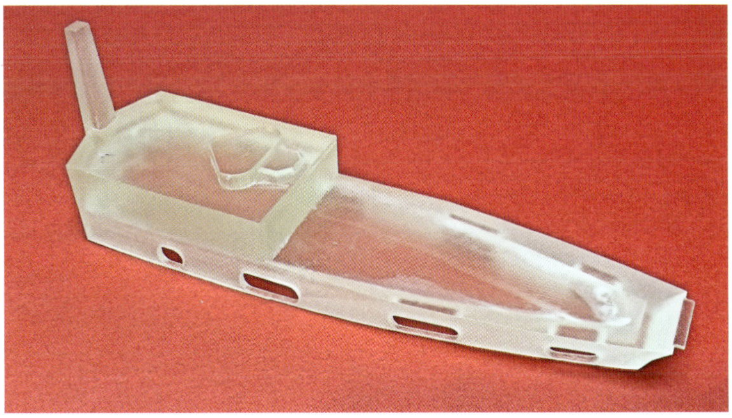

WHITE ENSIGN MODELS

1:350, 1:600 scales

The HMS *Belfast* etched set (PE35172) is for use with the 1:350 scale Trumpeter kit and comprises two large sheets. Sheet A includes pre-determined lengths of guardwires, together with inclined ladders, funnel grilles, radar antennas, details for the Walrus aircraft and for the pom-pom mounts. Sheet B includes the crane gantries, the catapult, parts for the boats, watertight doors and hatches, and details for the 4in gun mounts. When first released in the UK, WEM also produced a set (PRO 3536) containing a replacement compass platform and funnels. Sheet A of the etched brass included funnel grilles for both the kit funnels (which are too broad) and the corrected funnels.

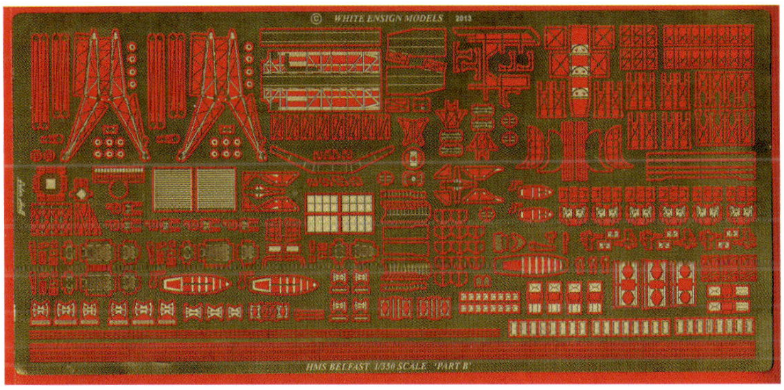

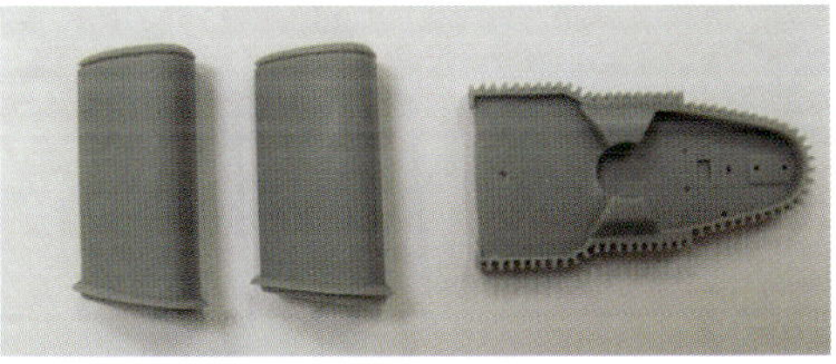

In 1999, whilst operating in the UK, White Ensign Models released a set of etched brass to 'super-detail' the Airfix kit of HMS *Belfast* (PE615). The set included two sheets, one containing generic guard-wires, and the other dedicated to this vessel. This set, now available from the USA, combines both sheets into one. The two main items were the crane jib and the catapult assembly. There were also radar antennas, fittings for the superstructure, funnel grilles, yardarms, boat supports, ladders, anchor chains, and watertight doors and hatches. Armament was not forgotten with both the 20mm Oerlikon guns and pom-pom mountings being included. Many modellers consider these to be only 'two-dimensional', and they can be replaced with newer 3D printed parts.

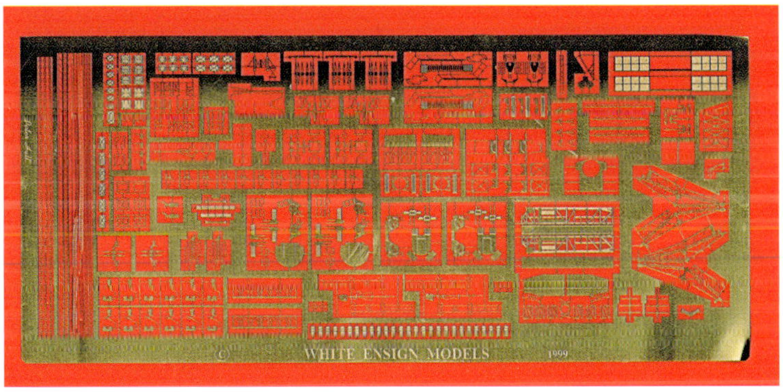

ATLANTIC MODELS

1:415, 1:600, 1:700 scales

In 2021, Atlantic Models also released an etched brass detail sheet for the Airfix *Belfast* kit (ATEM 60019). As both the masters for the WEM and Atlantic Models sets were produced by Peter Hall, it is not surprising that this is similar to that from WEM, but it is more extensive. One difference is that the guardwires are supplied in pre-determined lengths to match individual locations. Various lengths of inclined ladders are also provided for specific locations. The second main difference is the inclusion of lattice masts to assist the production of a model of *Belfast* post-war. Included are the various platforms and sensors.

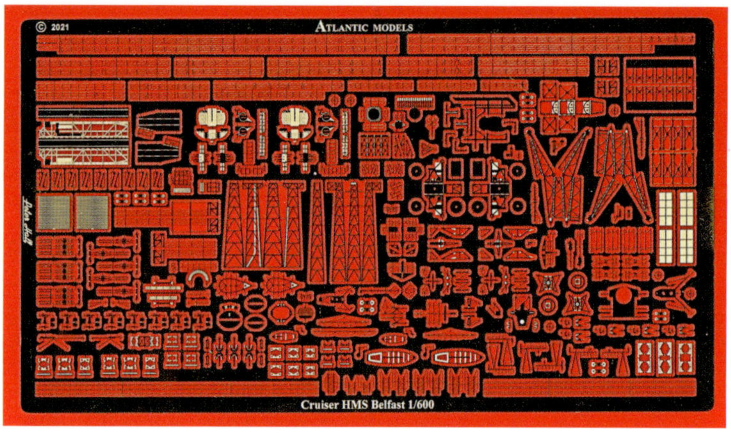

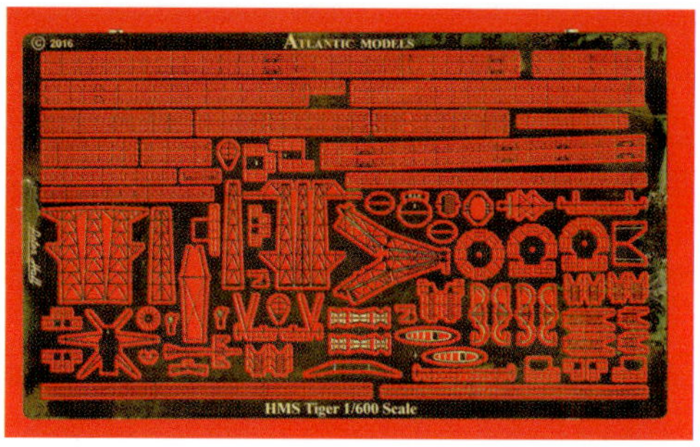

Both sets include the crane jibs, but the set from Atlantic Models also includes the cabs. Although this set does not include any watertight doors or hatches, it does offer the modeller greater detail, and opportunities to produce models of the vessel at different times in her career.

A set of photo-etch for *Tiger* was originally produced at 1:415 scale by WEM in the UK; it is still available from WEM in the USA as PE4017. The original was created by Peter Hall, who has enhanced the sheet and released it under the name of Atlantic Models (ATEMisc 04).

As well as the usual guardwires and ladders, the most noticeable parts are those supplied for the lattice masts, including all the necessary yardarms and platforms. The crane jib is also supplied, as are the boat davits and details for the boats, and a number of watertight doors of different patterns. A nice touch is the inclusion of nameplates for all three vessels in the class (*Lion*, *Tiger* and *Blake*) to be attached to the superstructure.

The sheet ATEM60004 for the Airfix *Tiger* kit contains many similar parts to that on the one above, but does not contain any watertight doors. The guardwires are produced in various lengths to match the kit, rather than generic lengths that need to be cut. There are some additional parts, including the gun director platforms and the aft funnel antenna spreader.

The main differences with the sheet at 1:700 scale, (ATEM70002), are the addition of parts related to the helicopter, including the rotor, flight deck netting and the stern catwalk. Additions also include the Type 965 radar antenna. There are also some detail changes, including different davits for the boats.

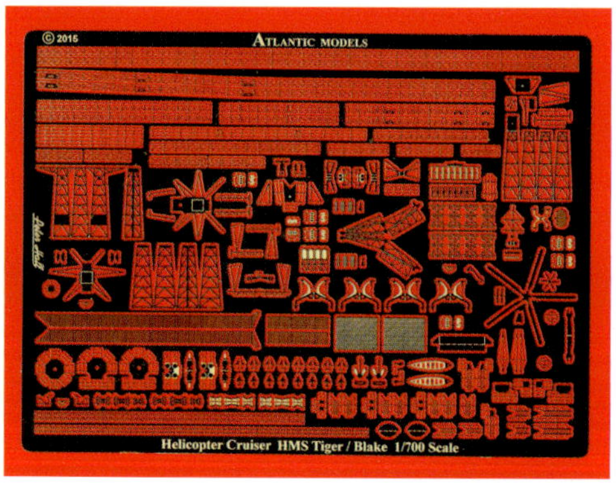

ARTWOXMODEL

1:600 scale

ArtwoxModel, from China, produce a self-adhesive wooden deck for the Airfix kit of *Belfast* (AW400241). It comprises eight shaped areas, with cutouts for bollards, etc. This is useful for the decks when bare wood, but they were, at times, overpainted.

A short length of brass anchor chain is included, and instructions are provided on a double-sided sheet of A4 paper.

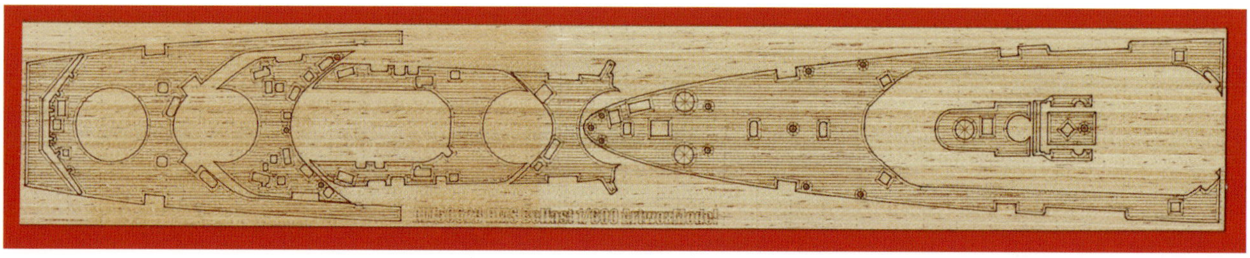

EDUARD

1:350 scale

The Czechia company of Eduard produce two sheets of etched brass and a small sheet of film which includes the glazing for the bridge windows (53210) for *Belfast*. Instructions are limited to 3½ sheets of A4 paper, which does not include an identity list of the parts. There are the usual parts for the cranes and catapult, with details for the armament, including shields for the twin 4in gun mountings, parts for the boats and watertight doors that can be displayed either open or closed. No guardwires or ladders are included, although these are available on generic sheets. The lack of clear identities for all the parts makes this set difficult to use.

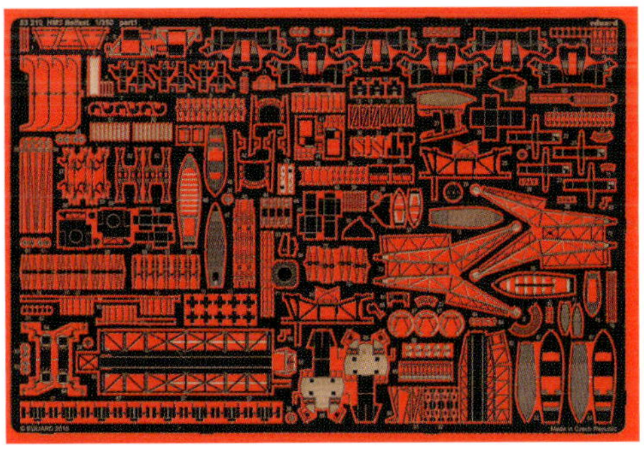

FLYHAWK

1:350 scale

The Flyhawk detail set for *Belfast* (FH 350117) includes sixteen sheets of etched brass, brass gun barrels and some resin components, including replacement funnels and compass platform. There are six sheets of instruction which require careful study to make optimum use of the set.

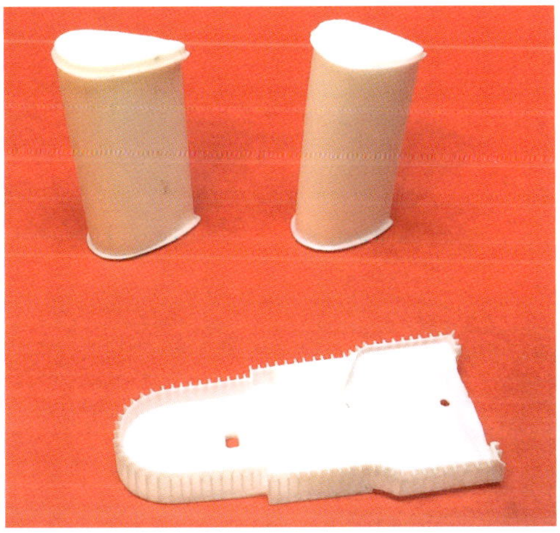

There are details for the various gun mounts, including the primary turret tops. The central barrel is different to the outer two in order to provide the required stagger of the muzzles when installed on the plastic mount. There are also boat details, cranes, radar antennas, details for the Walrus aircraft, the aircraft catapult, bridge details, lockers, carley floats, watertight doors, platform supports, ladders, guardwires, cable drum supports, davits and the breakwater and forecastle. The resin parts include deck vents.

WOOD HUNTER

1:350 scale

As well as a self-adhesive deck (in five parts), this American manufactured pack for *Belfast* (W35014) includes a short length of brass anchor chain and a small etched brass sheet containing cordage reel supports and two lockers, which the instructions show should be fitted on the quarterdeck. As well as the five deck sections, two for the maindeck and three for the superstructure, the sheet also includes four decks for the boats.

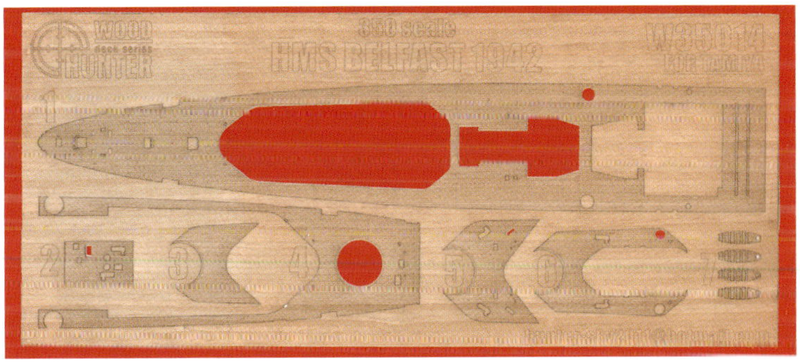

CHUANYU MODEL SHIP

1:700 scale

This self-adhesive wooden deck for *Belfast* is provided in two sections for the main deck, and two sections for the superstructure. In addition, there is a length of black anchor chain.

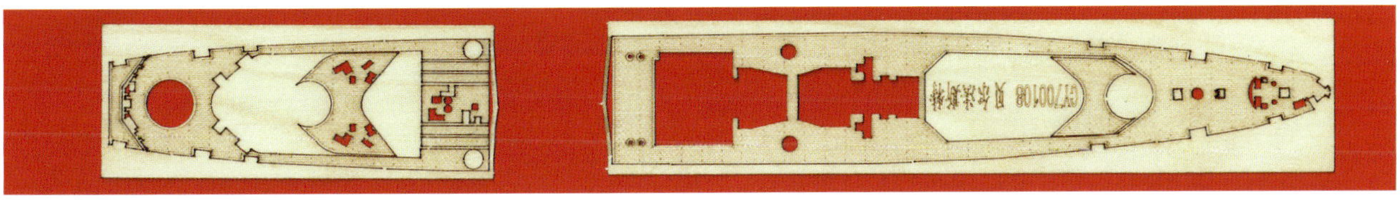

Modelmakers' Showcase

AIRFIX *BELFAST* 1:600 scale

By CHRIS HEWITT

Chris built his first *Belfast* some 40 years ago when it was first released in the 1970s by Airfix. This is his second go, but this time with photo-etch from White Ensign Models and wooden deck from Artwox. Not wanting to do camouflage, Chris had to determine when she went back to standard grey, but still based on the model. After some research he discovered she went out to the Far East just as the war in the Pacific was coming to a close – by this time the Walrus float plane had been removed and extra anti-aircraft armament had been fitted – but *Belfast* was back to being grey with the blue band on the hull.

This was one of the first models to have a guideline on the inside of the hull to mark the model waterline. The wooden deck is a very thin veneer, which saves a lot of time, but care must be taken putting it down, so you need to take it slowly. Chris wanted brass barrels and there was nothing on the market so he took the chance and bought from Master Barrels 8in instead of 6in; because of differences between 1/600 and 1/700, they looked right.

The main alteration to *Belfast* was the relocation of the ship's boats and the

Anatomy of the Ship: The Cruiser Belfast by Ross Watton came in very handy, page 72 showing all the changes, including the armament.

Chris still wanted a Walrus in the display and found out some were retained on aircraft carriers, so that's a Walrus arriving with the mail.

L'ARSENAL *SHEFFIELD* & WEM *SHEFFIELD* 1:700 scale

By DAVE EYLES

These two models were built simultaneously to compare the different approaches used by the two manufacturers when casting the resin components. The L'Arsenal kit was the early issue, with no 3D printed parts included.

The conclusion was that although the two kits did present different challenges, they were of similar complexity and difficulty and the resulting models were of similar quality. The L'Arsenal kit is identified by the carley floats on the quarterdeck, which does illustrate some detail differences between the two kits.

TRUMPETER *BELFAST* 1:350 scale

By IAN RUSCOE

Ian used the etched brass and accessory set from White Ensign Models to correct and enhance the Trumpeter kit. He also added a considerable number of figures, not only in their work stations, such as on the bridge, but also relaxing on the quarter-deck.

The model is painted in the camouflage pattern worn when *Belfast* was operating in Northern Waters, in August 1943.

HMS BELFAST
NORTHERN WATERS, AUGUST 1943

AIRFIX ***NIGERIA*** 1:600 scale

By ARY MOORE

Ary's father served aboard *Nigeria* from commissioning to being dropped off in Charleston when the ship went in for repairs after being torpedoed on Operation Pedestal. After a stint on *Glasgow* he returned to *Nigeria* and saw out the war on board her. After retiring, Ary wanted to build a model of *Nigeria* and spotted a couple of articles on kit conversions. He obtained an old Airfix *Tiger* kit as a base.

Ary already had a *Belfast* kit as a parts donor but some of these were eventually replaced with 3D printed and PE parts. The main suppliers were MicroMaster both from its own site and the Shapeways market place. The 'Colony' class turret set, carley floats, searchlights, Oerlikon guns, quad Vickers and additional boats were all purchased. He also had some triple torpedo mounts, but unless they are fitted swung out for action they do not add anything as the torpedo man's sidecar is obscured by the gun deck in the housed position. He also had some gun tubs, bollards, cleats and quad pom-poms from Shapeways. The medium used for these is quite brittle and there were a few casualties just removing them from the sprue.

The funnels and the large angled vent between the hangars were designed by Martyn Denchfield and printed by James at Triple Axis. Martyn also supplied a guide to official navy paint colours. The photo-etch used came from the *Belfast* set plus some additional doors, all supplied by Peter Hall at Atlantic Models. Nigel Denchfield supplied dimensions from a model he had built previously and the formula for scaling the Raven & Roberts drawing. The author provided the camouflage patterns and colour palette.

REVELL *TIGER* 1:700 scale

By CHRIS HEWITT

Chris has always liked the gun version of the *Tiger* class and at last he was able to build one, now that 3D printing from Shapeways and photo-etch from Atlantic Models, which covers both versions of the *Tiger* class, were available. There are two kits on the market, one released by Matchbox in 1979 and the Revell kit of 2012, which is from the same moulds. Chris managed to buy the Matchbox kit at a very reasonable price.

First he had to cut the hanger part off, which went well, and with this off, he could fit the stern superstructure which is a 3D part also from Shapeways. Chris had spare wooden deck which was needed for the quarter deck. Shapeways also provide a set which includes 2 x 6in turrets and 3 x 3in turrets plus lot of parts produced by Bogeys Bits. The junks are 1/700 kits by Rainbow. Rigging is from 'Rig that Thing', which Chris highly recommends. Brass barrels from Master, the display case is by Trumpeter, and the figures are from Eduard.

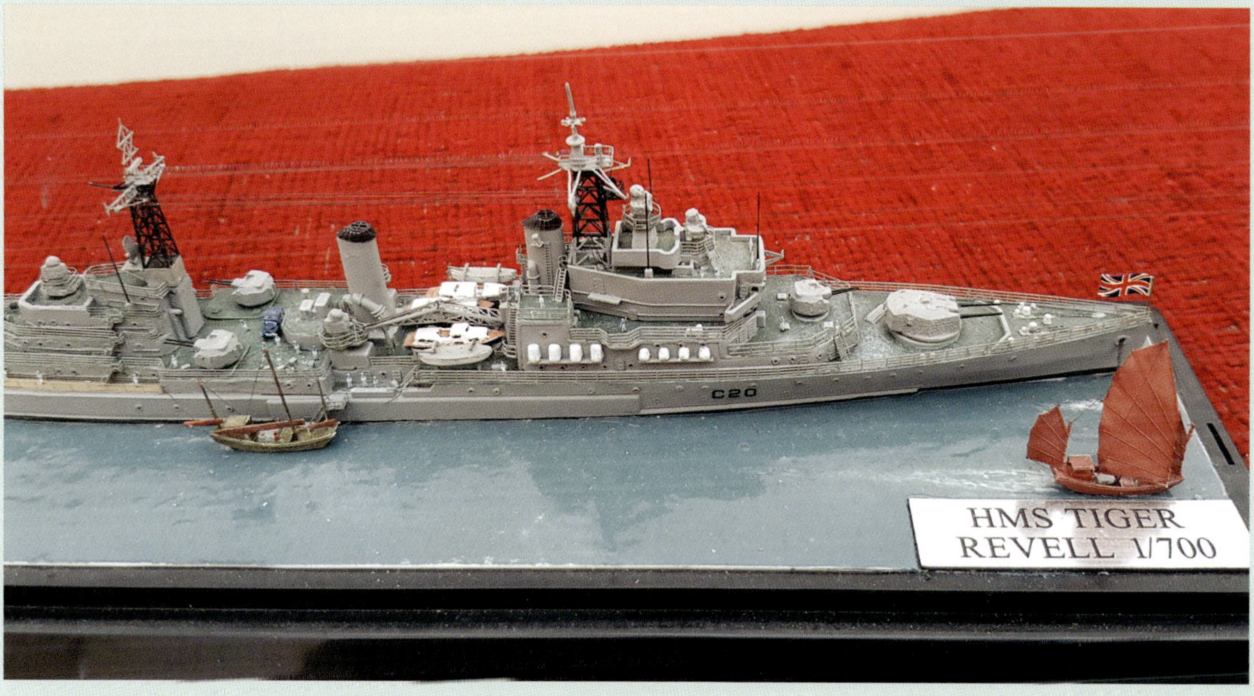
C20
HMS TIGER
REVELL 1/700

C20

WHITE ENSIGN MODELS *SHEFFIELD* 1:350 scale

By MIKE McCABE

Mike was an experienced, keen ship modeller for many years, winning a number of awards in competitions, before he started Starling Models, and this experience is evident in both the products the company produces and the products selected for sale by the company but produced by others.

This model was built from the White Ensign kit, and Mike has portrayed it in a realistic seascape, one of his specialities. The model is also fully rigged, and painted in a complex camouflage pattern that she wore for a period during World War II.

HMS Sheffield

HMS Sheffield

L'ARSENAL *GAMBIA* & WEM *SHEFFIELD* 1:700 scale By PETER FULGONEY

Gambia and *Sheffield* appear on the dust jacket of the Raven & Roberts book *British Cruisers of World War Two* which gave Peter the inspiration to build these two kits in diorama and as shown in that illustration. The model includes the L'Arsenal *Gambia*, a resin and photo-etch kit, together with the White Ensign Models *Sheffield*. Constructing these two side by side creates an interesting comparison between the older and more modern interpretations; however, the building of one did support the other with the WEM photo-etch being Peter's preferred choice, but the extensive detailing on the L'Arsenal kit is exceptional.

Having a spare photo-etch of the WEM *Edinburgh* did make the difference and so Peter was able to make his presentation without too many tears. Both kits have pros and cons and so in conclusion there is no one favourite and in fact one supports the other.

As a modelling guide, all the paint colours are available and well illustrated for both kits. The rigging is fairly basic and Peter used stretched sprue, 0.06mm wire and 'Rig that Thing' to complete his presentation. As usual with these WWII builds, Peter left the 281 radar configurations until last, preferring the WEM photo-etch to finish.

FROG *TIGER* 1:415 scale

By KEITH JONES

With this model, Keith shows what can be achieved from a basic kit, a few aftermarket parts, some skill and a lot of patience. With there being no other large-scale kits of these handsome vessels available, this unusual scale had to be used but, fortunately, the aftermarket suppliers had recognised the desire of many modellers to build large, high quality models of this class of cruisers.

Many would say that the modification to include a hangar and flightdeck, carried out on two of the class, created 'ugly ducklings', but for those who wish to model the vessels in this state, it is necessary to work in the smaller scales of either 1:700 or, using aftermarket components, 1:600 – or undertake a scratch-build.

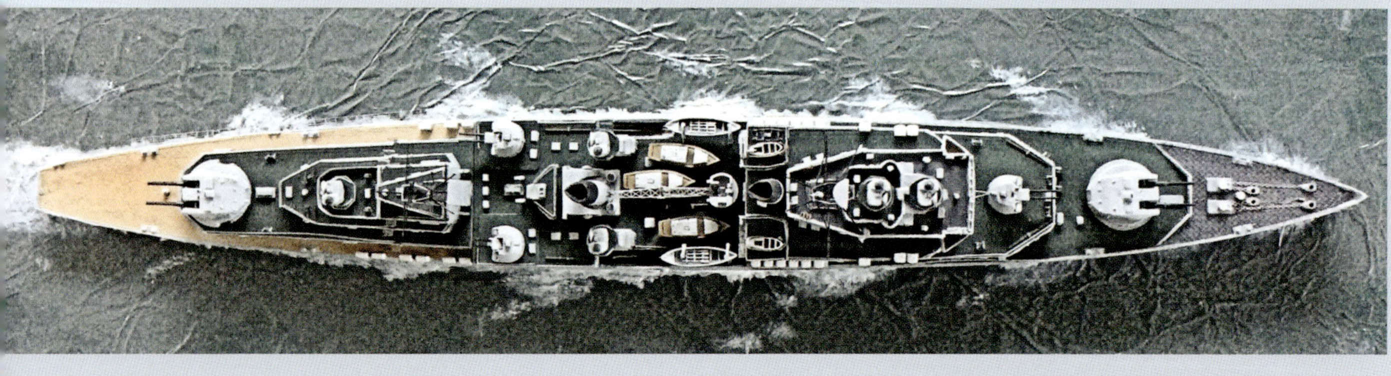

C20

C20

AIRFIX *BELFAST* 1:600 scale

By KEITH BUTTERLEY

The Airfix *Belfast* kit was first released in 1973, and today it is still a very accurate and detailed kit, truly one of Airfix's better efforts. With the appearance of White Ensign Models Photo-Etch fret for the *Belfast*, one can now make a good model even better.

Keith decided that he would make the *Belfast* a waterline model, and started by taping the hull along and below the boot top. Using a razor saw, he cut along the top of the tape, and then glued the hull halves together before sanding. The decks must be installed before sanding in order to prevent the hull from bowing during sanding. Chris uses a Plexiglas fluorescent light panel for his base, a type called 'cracked ice'. He then took the hull and traced around it with a marking pen on the flat surface of the panel and cut a hole, remembering to cut inside the traced line. The few gaps were very small and were hardly noticeable when the hull was placed in the hole.

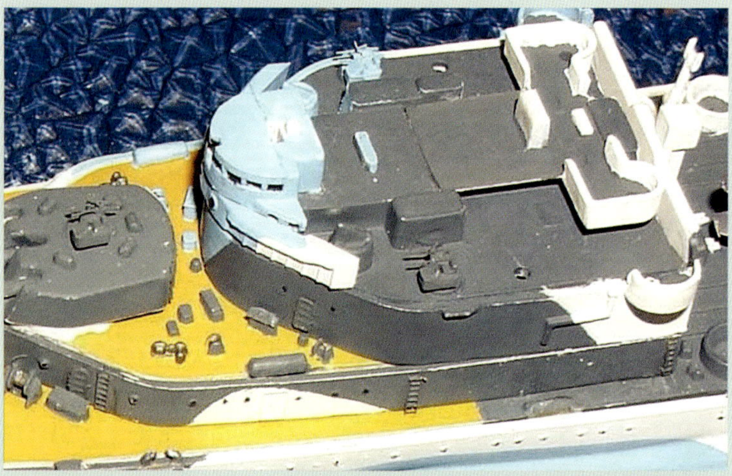

Chris was now ready to paint the wake, and taped the bow area in a 'V' to produce a hard line as the ship would be digging into the water here and the demarcation is very sharp. He sprayed Model Master Flat White FS37875 for the wash, making sure to give it that extra blast at the stern and feathering back for the wake, and then over sprayed with a couple coats of Model Master Blue Angel Blue FS15050.

He primed the hull with Model Master Light Gray FS36495 and applied the AP507C (Humbrol 147) over it, masked the pattern for B6 (Humbrol 68) next, then B5 (Humbrol 144) and finally the AP507A (Humbrol 112). To do the rust, Chris used a child's watercolour set, mixing green, black and orange, until the right colour was achieved.

The decks were fairly straightforward, but you do have to plan ahead. The PE catapult is a nifty little model in itself. The 6in gun turrets did not prove to be much of a problem, but do note there are two doors on the rear of the turrets, one at each side, with a ladder on the left side only, to the outside of the door. The fit of the superstructure parts was not exactly precise, leaving gaps to fill, and there were sinkholes that had to be filled.

The kits boats are terrible and should be replaced. The many resin and 3D printed accessories were not available when Chris built his model but he did replace the moulded-on boat chocks with PE ones. The kit 4in HA guns and eight-barrel pom-poms were replaced by WEM resin parts, and PE replaced the 20mm guns and crane booms.

Chris used 8X (.003) fly tying tippet for the rigging, giving it a wash of flat black paint and attaching it with Superglue, and then wrapped it all up by airbrushing with Testors Dullcote.

HMS *Edinburgh* 1939

507C

HMS *Gloucester* 1941

507 A 507 C

HMS *Edinburgh* 1942

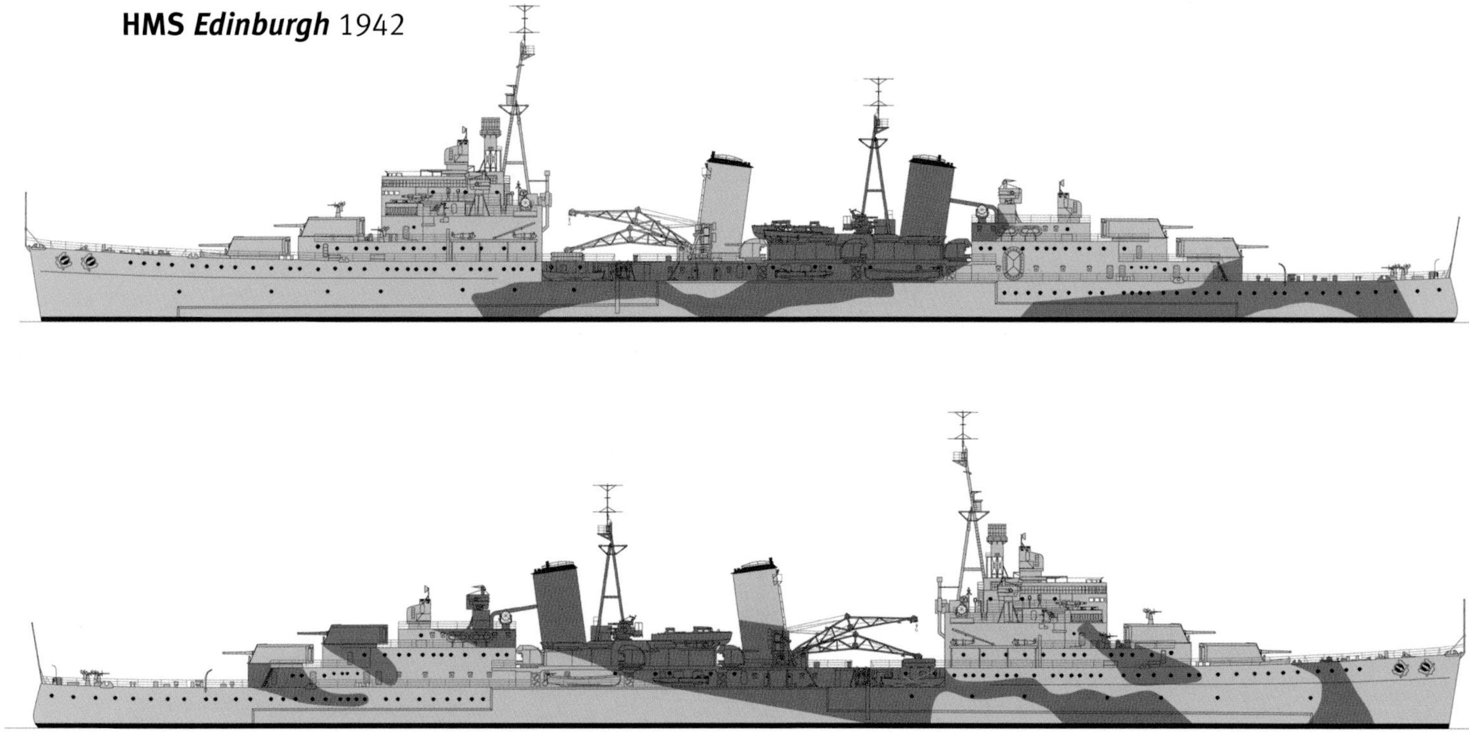

HMS *Sheffield* 1941

HMS *Mauritius* 1942

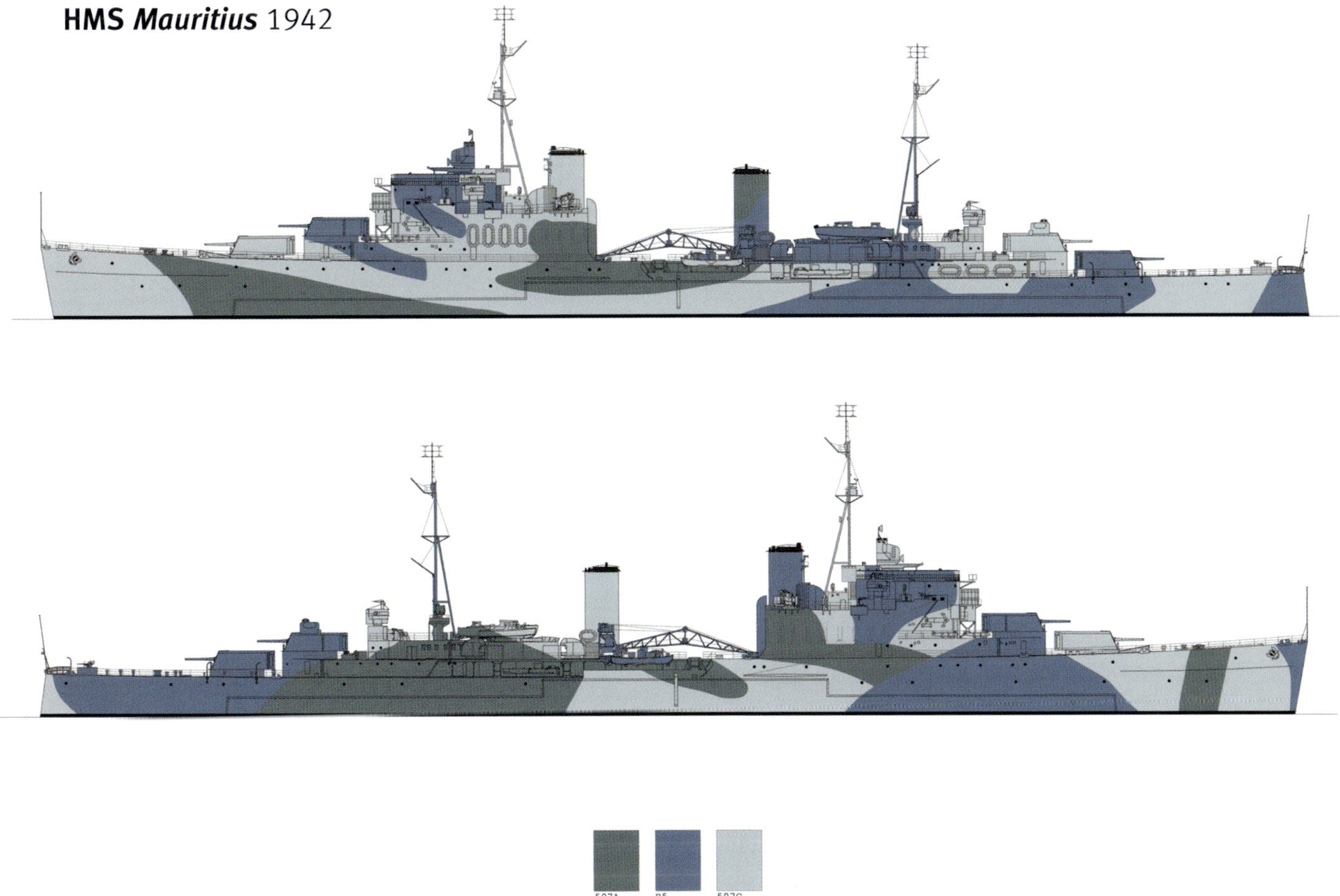

HMS *Ceylon* 1943

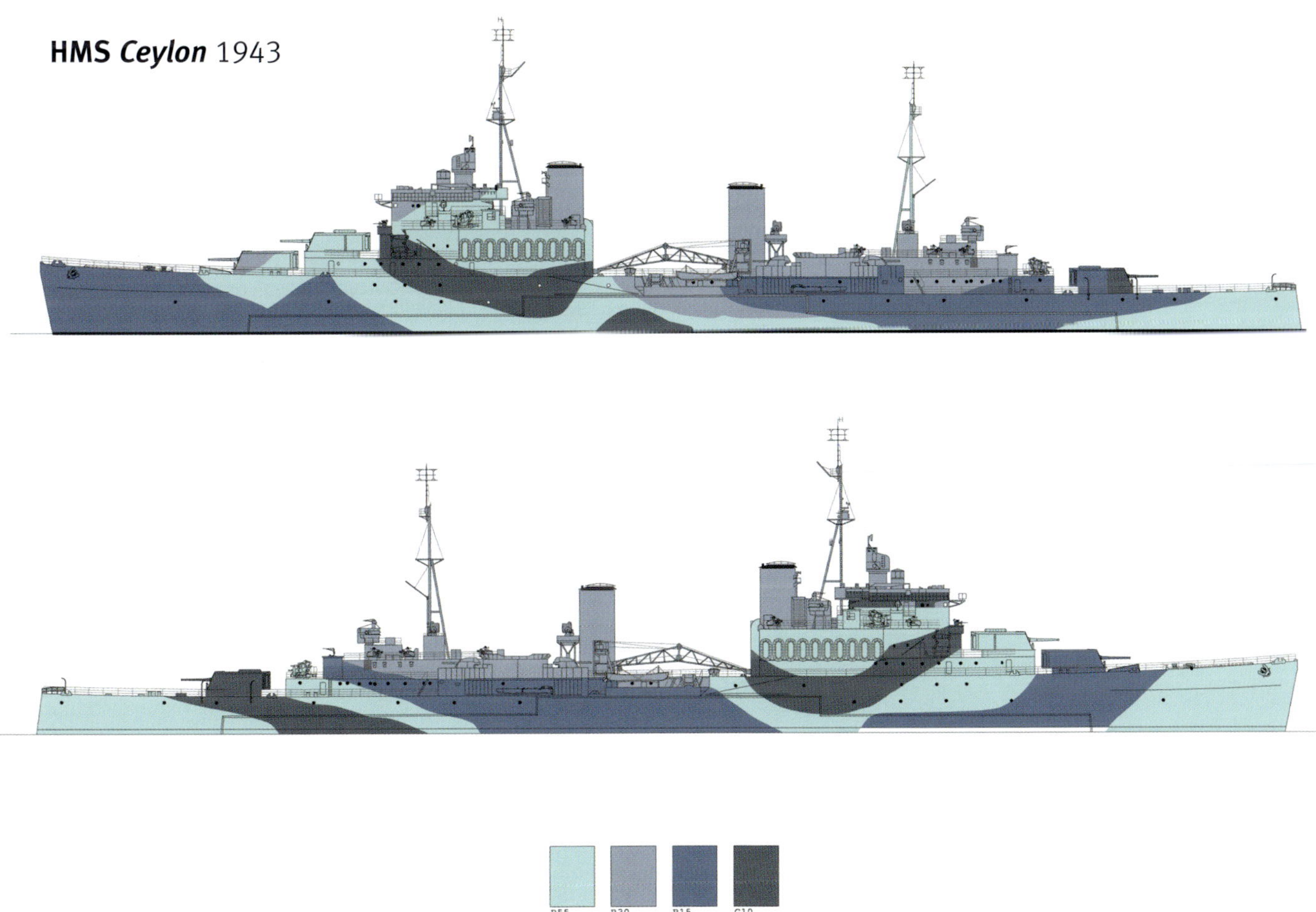

HMS *Manchester* 1942

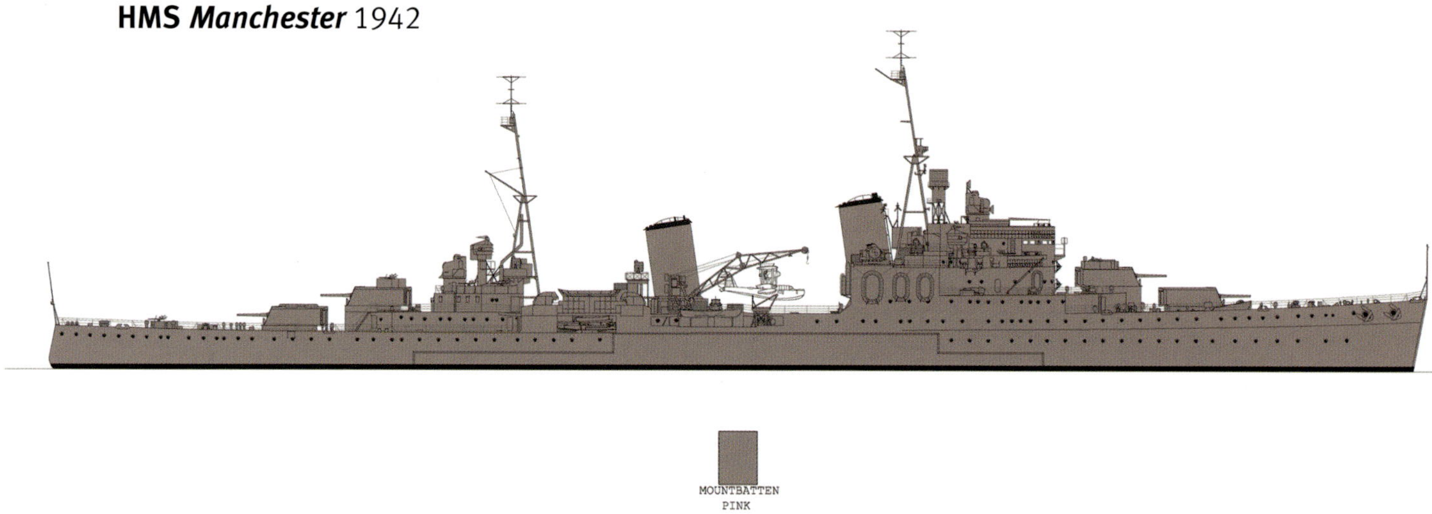

HMS *Gambia* 1942

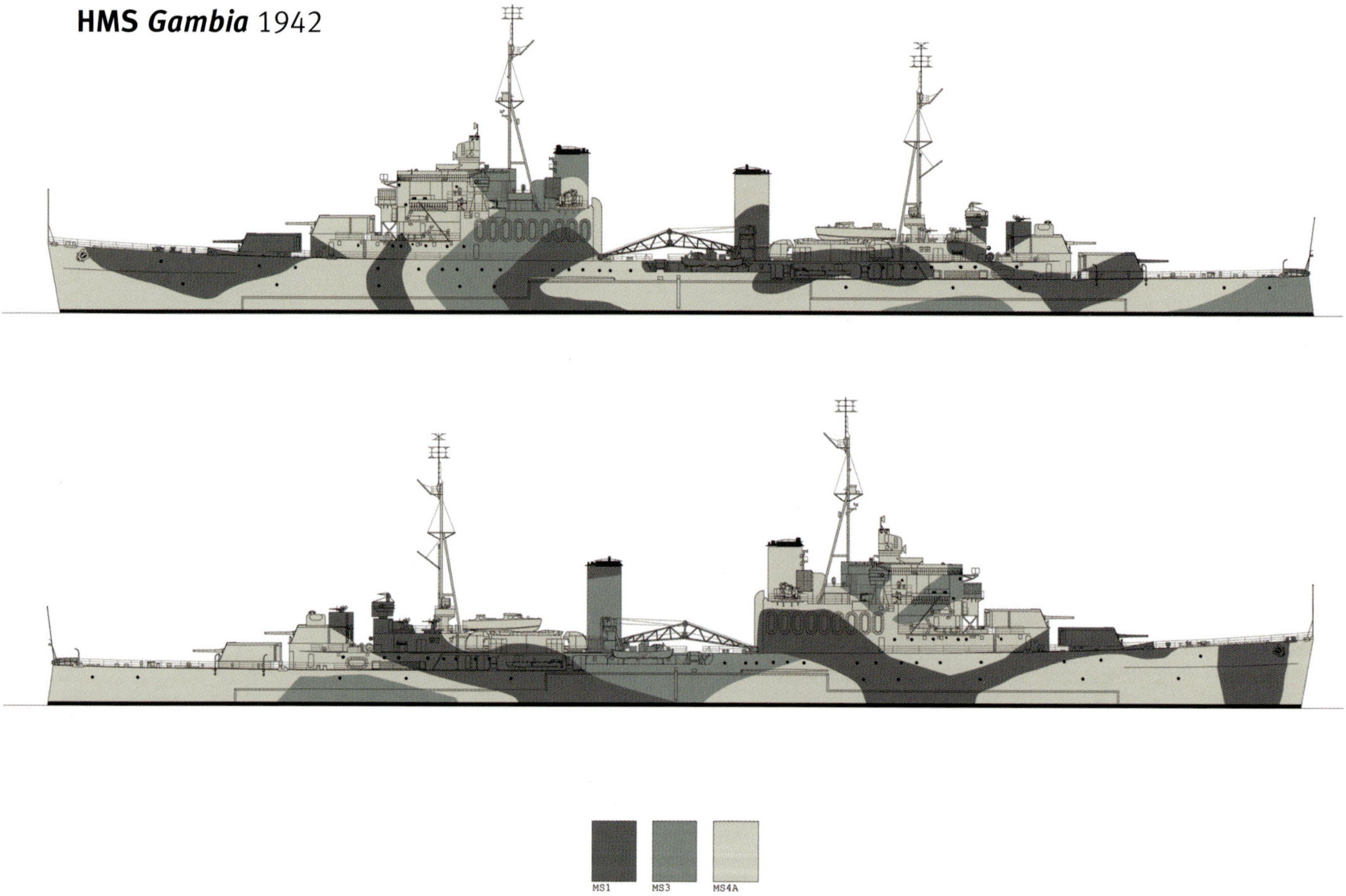

HMNZS *Gambia* 1945

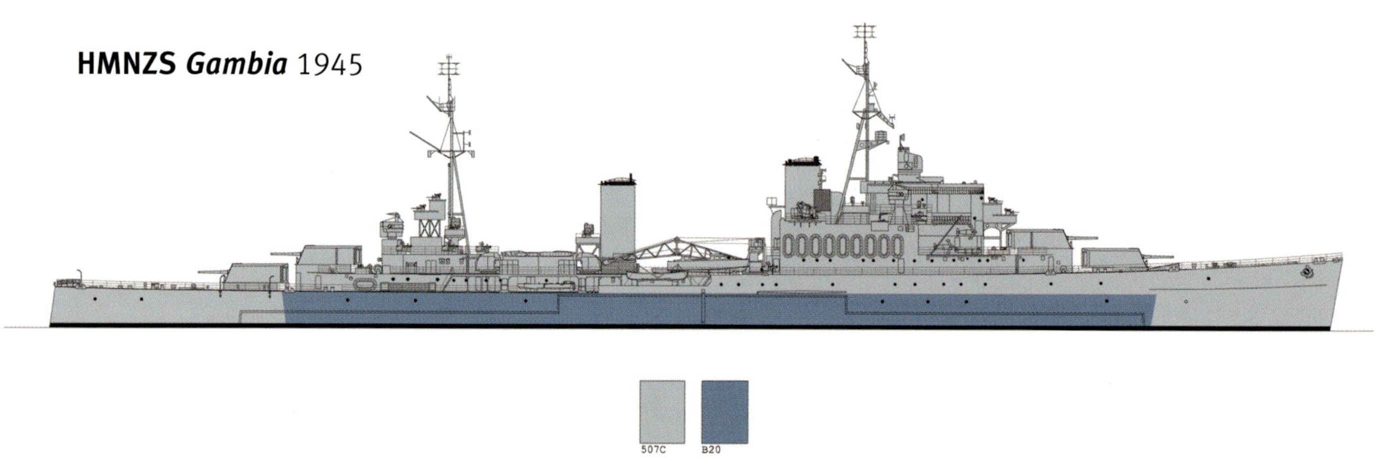

Camouflage

SOUTHAMPTON CLASS

Those vessels which served with the Home Fleet pre-war were painted MS4a overall. Wooden decks were scrubbed, with the metal decks also painted MS4a, except for the anchor-handling area, which was painted either 507a or 507b. Mast tops, above the tripod were painted white. During the Spanish Civil War, red-white-blue neutrality stripes were carried on 'B' and 'X' turrets, blue being the forward stripe on each turret.

While serving on the China station, *Birmingham* was painted white with grey 507b funnels. Wooden decks were scrubbed, with the metal decks also painted white, except for the anchor-handling area, which was painted either 507a or 507b. *Manchester* served on the East Indies station, where she was painted in the same colour scheme, apart from the funnels, which were buff. During 1939, her funnels were painted grey 507b.

Southampton. At the beginning of the war, *Southampton* was painted 507b. While based at Scapa Flow in 1940, she carried the unofficial 'Flotta' scheme of white, black, brown and green. This was intended to be effective against the land background, the hulls being primarily white, with the other colours on the upperworks. This scheme was only worn for a few weeks, and *Southampton* returned to 507b when she moved to the Mediterranean. She carried a painted white bow wave during the Battle of Spartivento, November 1940.

Sheffield. A crew member recalls *Sheffield* being painted in 507a, with a white triangle at the bow, during the early part of the war, but there is no photographic evidence of

This poor photograph of *Sheffield* illustrates the complexity of her first camouflage scheme.

this, and she was in 507b when she joined Force H in 1940. Whilst under repair in 1941, she received a very complicated Admiralty scheme, which included white, 507c, 507a, MS1, MS2 and B5. The colours continued on the deck and horizontal surfaces of the superstructure. In 1942, *Sheffield* was repainted in a much simpler intermediate disruptive scheme using just 507c, 507a and B5. Decks were dark grey. In October 1943, she received a paint scheme of G10 for the hull and decks, with B55 upperworks. During her refit in the USA, *Sheffield* received the standard Admiralty scheme of B20 hull and decks, including turret tops, and G45 upperworks. After the war, *Sheffield* served on the West Indies station, where she was painted in MS4a. Metal decks remained in B20, but wooden decks were restored to their pre-war scrubbed finish.

Newcastle. At the beginning of the war, *Newcastle* was painted 507b overall, except for areas of wooden deck. As part of Force H, she was painted MS4a, but with entire masts white. The forecastle deck and the top of 'B' turret were painted 507a. On her return from a refit in the USA at the end of 1941, she received an Admiralty scheme

Glasgow in August 1942, Statue of Liberty in the background, showing the simple rectangular blocks of colour worn at that time.

Liverpool at Mare Island, California, in October 1941.

using B5, 507c and B15. The pattern was the same on both sides. In 1943, the pattern was simplified and included just two colours, B5 and B15. Decks were dark grey. On transfer to the Eastern Fleet in 1943, she was painted overall in 507c, with a darker panel on her hull, stretching from before 'A' turret to aft of 'Y' turret. Decks and horizontal surfaces were 507a.

Birmingham. Remaining on the China station at the beginning of the war, *Birmingham* was painted 507b overall, including decks, apart from a few areas amidships on the superstructure and aft on the hull, which were painted 507c. Following her refit in Simonstown in 1942, she wore a four-colour scheme of MS4a with areas of G10, B5 and B6. Decks were dark grey, probably 507a, and masts were white above the tripod section. During her refit in mid-1943, she was painted G45, with areas of G10 and B30. Decks and masts were unchanged. In 1944, *Birmingham* adopted the standard scheme of MS3, with a hull panel and decks G10.

Glasgow. At the beginning of the war, *Glasgow* was painted 507a, with the decks remaining bare wood and MS4a. While under repair in Singapore in 1941, she received a scheme of 507c with rectangles of 507a, the decks being painted the same colour as the sides, except where wooden.

GLOUCESTER CLASS

Liverpool. When *Liverpool* went to the Mediterranean in 1940, she was painted in 507c, with contrasting areas of 507a. The pattern was the same on both sides, and her metal decks were 507a, the wooden ones remaining unpainted. On her return to Great Britain after repairs in the USA (late 1941), she was painted in the same colours, with additional areas of B5, but to a very different pattern. Following further damage, she did not recommission until 1945, when her hull was painted 507b, with 507c upperworks. Metal surfaces were 507a, and wooden areas were unpainted.

Manchester. *Manchester* entered the war painted 507b overall, with wooden deck areas. Operating in the Mediterranean in late 1940, she was painted light Mountbatten Pink, with 507b decks, the wooden areas remaining unpainted. After a refit in early 1941, she was painted 507b all over, with white tops to her masts. When lost, she was once again in Mountbatten Pink.

Gloucester. During her time in the Mediterranean, *Gloucester* was painted 507c, with areas of 507a for contrast. These areas were defined by straight lines. Decks were painted 507b, with wooden areas stained to match. Turret tops were 507a, apart from that of 'B' turret, which was white.

EDINBURGH CLASS

Belfast. Following major repairs, *Belfast* returned to service in 1942 painted in a four-colour scheme of 507a, 507c, B5 and B6. Horizontal metal surfaces were 507a. By the time of the Battle of North Cape, B6

Belfast in 1942 (top), and *Edinburgh* (bottom) in the camouflage pattern she was wearing at the time of her loss.

Starboard profile of *Nigeria* in June 1943.

was no longer used, and the areas had changed quite significantly, although the overall appearance was the same. As a museum ship, she is painted in a scheme which resembles that carried in 1944, although her configuration is as decommissioned. Prepared for operations in the Pacific, *Belfast* was painted 507c, with a hull panel of B15.

Edinburgh. During the early part of the war, *Edinburgh* was painted 507b overall, with the exception of the forecastle area, which was 507a, and the bare wooden decks. Shortly before her loss, she received a three-colour scheme of 507a and B5 on a base of 507c. Decks were 507b, with the exception of the wooden quarterdeck.

FIJI CLASS

Nigeria. During the early years of the war, *Nigeria* was painted in Mountbatten Pink, a medium shade for the hull and a lighter shade for the upperworks. Horizontal surfaces were 507b, except for the wooden decks. In mid-1941, she carried an experimental scheme of large areas of MS2 on 507c, for a short time. She returned to medium Mountbatten Pink overall. At the end of the year, and into early 1942, *Nigeria* was painted 507c, with areas of B5 and MS1, these colours being continued over the decks. Later in 1942, the scheme was changed but used the same colours. The pattern was changed again in mid-1943, once again retaining the same colours, but by the end of the year, *Nigeria* was painted in 507b for the hull, and B55 for the upperworks. In 1944, she was 507c overall, with a B5 hull panel.

After her sale to India, when she was renamed *Mysore*, she was painted 507a, or similar.

This starboard bow view of *Mauritius* in 1942 shows the camouflage pattern off clearly.

Jamaica in September 1943, with her freshly painted camouflage scheme.

Fiji. On completion, *Fiji* was painted 507b overall, with the forecastle area 507a. After repairs in early 1941, she appeared in a scheme using 507a, 507b and 507c. Horizontal surfaces were 507b, with the exception of wooden areas.

Mauritius. *Mauritius* was completed in 507c, with areas of 507a added soon after. Decks were wood and 507b. The pattern was modified during 1941, and after her refit in 1942, *Mauritius* appeared in a three-colour scheme of 507c, with areas of 507b and black. The main deck was 507a, with a forecastle area of 507b. The forward superstructure deck was 507c, as was the hangar top, with the after decks being 507a. Turret tops were 507b, with the exception of 'A' turret, which was 507c. The quarterdeck was wood. After repairs in 1943, she had a 507b hull and decks with 507c upperworks. At the end of the war, *Mauritius* was painted 507c with a B5 hull panel, with 507b horizontal surfaces.

Trinidad. During her short career, *Trinidad* carried a four-colour scheme of B5, MS1, B30 and B55. Metal decks were 507b, with wooden areas.

Kenya. *Kenya* entered service in a two-tone Mountbatten Pink camouflage scheme, using light and dark shades. Decks were probably 507b, with turret tops matching the hull side colours. In autumn 1941, she was light Mountbatten Pink with 507b decks and turret tops. In May 1942, she had a dark Mountbatten Pink hull and parts of the superstructure, with the remainder in the light shade, apart from 'A' turret which was white. In the middle of the year, *Kenya* was dark Mountbatten Pink overall, with the exception of a small area near the bow, which was light. After repairs later in 1942, she wore MS4 and MS4a. Decks were 507a, as were the tops of 'A' and 'X' turrets, the other two being 507b. When *Kenya* joined the Eastern Fleet in 1944, she was 507c overall with a B5 hull panel. Decks and turret tops were 507a.

Immediately after the war, *Kenya* had a MS4a hull and 507c upperworks. This was soon changed to 507c overall. Decks were 507b, with wooden areas.

Jamaica. *Jamaica* was commissioned with a four-colour scheme of 507c, B5, B6 and MS1. The wooden quarterdeck was unpainted, with 507a metal decks. The tops

Kenya with a dark hull and dark patches on the superstructure.

Gambia in 1942.

of 'A' and 'B' turrets were 507c, 'X' turret MS1 and 'Y' turret B6. In 1943, she received an unusual scheme of 507c, with areas of blue-green. When *Jamaica* returned from her modernisation at the end of the war, she was 507c overall, with a B5 hull panel.

Post-war, *Jamaica* retained 507c overall, with black masts and 507b decks, apart from wooden areas. The forecastle area was painted Brunswick green.

Gambia. *Gambia* entered service painted in a scheme of MS2, MS3 and MS4a, with a wooden quarterdeck and other areas painted 507b. The tops of 'X' and 'Y' turrets were MS2, 'B' turret MS3 and 'A' turret MS4. The catapult deck was MS2. On transfer to New Zealand in 1943, she was painted in B10, B15, B30 and B55, with 507b decks and turret tops, apart from the wooden quarterdeck. On joining the Eastern Fleet in early 1944, her hull was 507b with 507c upperworks. The decks remained unchanged. In the middle of that year, she received a B5 hull panel, with the remainder of the ship painted 507c (some sources show 507a). Decks and turret tops were 507b, except for the wooden quarterdeck. On joining the British Pacific Fleet in 1945, *Gambia* was painted MS4a, with a B15 hull panel.

Returning to RN service after the war, she was painted 507c, with 507b horizontal surfaces, and a wooden quarterdeck. For a while, the forecastle was painted Brunswick Green.

Bermuda. On completion, *Bermuda* carried an Admiralty light disruption scheme of MS4a, MS2 and MS3. Decks were painted grey, possibly 507b, with the forecastle in 507a. The turret tops of 'X' and 'Y' turrets were MS2, while those of 'A' and 'B' were MS4a. In the autumn of 1943, the scheme was simplified slightly and used MS4, MS4a and MS2, the decks remaining as before. On completion of her refit in early 1944, her hull was painted entirely in MS4.

Following the removal of 'X' turret, *Bermuda*'s hull was painted MS4 and the upperworks 507c. A blue panel, B5, was added to the hull in mid-1945.

UGANDA CLASS

Ceylon. On completion, *Ceylon* was painted in G10, B15, B30 and B55, with Semtex decks. Other horizontal surfaces were B30 with the exception of the turret tops, which were G10 for the forward pair of turrets and B55 for the single one aft. On joining the Eastern Fleet in 1944, she was painted 507c overall, with a B5 hull panel. The decks were still Semtex and other horizontal surfaces were painted B30. When *Ceylon* joined the British Pacific Fleet in 1945, she was painted MS3 overall, with a B20 hull panel. Decks and horizontal surfaces remained as before. She returned to the Eastern Fleet, and the colour scheme in 1945, but the hull panel was lighter.

After the war, she was painted in MS4a, with black masts. Deck colours varied but she almost certainly had a dull red forecastle and Brunswick green decks for some of the time. These colours remained after her reconstruction, which included lattice masts.

Uganda. In RN service, *Uganda* wore a camouflage scheme of 507a, 507b and

Ceylon in 1943, note the array of carley floats on the side of the forward superstructure.

Newfoundland leaving the Tyne in January 1943.

507c, but on transfer to Canada in 1944, she was MS4a overall, with a B5 hull panel. White counter-shading was used below the knuckle at the bow. Renamed *Quebec* after the war, she operated as a training ship, with a 507b hull and MS4a superstructure.

Newfoundland. On entry into service, *Newfoundland* wore a camouflage scheme of 507a over 507c. Decks were Semtex and other horizontal surfaces 507a. After repairs in the United States, in 1944 she wore a temporary camouflage scheme for a few months. This consisted primarily of MS4 and B30. She joined the Eastern Fleet in 1945 and was painted 507c with a B5 hull panel. Apart from the Semtex decks, horizontal surfaces were 507a. White was used for counter-shading. Later in the year, her hull panel was changed to B20. During late operations against Japan, *Newfoundland* was painted MS3 overall, with a B15 hull panel. She retained the white counter-shading under the knuckle at the bow.

MINOTAUR CLASS

Minotaur. Completed too late for the war in Europe, HMCS *Ontario* (as she was renamed) was painted 507c with a blue hull panel. Decks were 507a and turret tops were 507c.

Swiftsure. *Swiftsure* completed in a dark scheme of G10, B15, G45 and MS3. Decks were B5 but other horizontal surfaces matched the colour of the adjoining upright surface. On joining the British Pacific Fleet, she adopted MS3 overall, with a B15 hull panel. Decks and horizontal surfaces were B5, with the exception of the top of 'B' turret, which was MS3. Counter-shading was applied under the knuckle.

Superb. Completed too late for the war, *Superb* was painted MS4a overall, with 507b metal surfaces. Being unplanked, her decks were Semtex, which was painted Brunswick green.

Ontario wearing the blue hull panel.

Post-war

TIGER CLASS

Two more cruisers, *Tiger* and *Defence*, were also authorised under the 1941 supplementary programme, and a further two, *Hawke* and *Blake*, under the 1942 programme. Shortly after being ordered, *Tiger* was renamed *Bellerophon*, and laid down in August 1944. Renamed *Blake* and then renamed *Bellerophon* once again, she was cancelled in March 1946. *Defence* was suspended in 1946. *Hawke* was suspended in 1945 and cancelled in 1946, subsequently being broken-up. *Blake*, briefly renamed *Tiger* before returning to her original name, was suspended in 1946.

The three remaining cruisers, *Tiger*, *Defence* and *Blake*, did not resume construction until 1954, to a completely revised design. *Defence* was subsequently renamed *Lion* in 1957. The modernisation was very extensive. It involved stripping out all the superstructure, bridge and gun supports and replacing most of the existing internal fittings. During the extended build, the appearance of the ships was changed significantly, and the machinery was uprated to produce 80,000shp, giving a maximum speed of 31.5 knots.

Originally intended to retain nine 6in guns in three turrets and ten 4in guns in five mounts, with enhanced close-in armament, the three surviving vessels emerged with just four 6in guns in two twin Mk 26 turrets, and six 3in guns, in three twin Mk 6 turrets. The 6in guns were capable of firing at up to 20 rounds per minute per barrel and the 3in theoretically at up to 120 rounds per minute, although 90 was the maximum achieved. The Mk 26 turret had an elevation range of -5° to +80° and the Mk 6 turret a range of -15° to +90°. Both main and secondary weapons were directed by the radar-equipped MRS3 fire control system. Each gun mounting had its own radar-equipped director, meaning that it was possible to engage up to five targets at the same time.

TIGER CLASS BUILDING DATA

Name	Builder	Laid down	Launched
Tiger (ex-*Bellerophon*)	John Brown	01.10.1941	25.10.1945
Lion (ex-*Defence*)	Scotts (until launch) Swan Hunter (completion)	22.09.1941	04.02.1943
Blake (ex-*Tiger*, ex-*Blake*)	Fairfield	17.08.1942	20.12.1945

Internally, the ships benefitted from modern command and control facilities and a limited degree of protection against nuclear, biological and chemical contamination. Crew facilities were upgraded from traditional 'broadside messing' to the latest cafeteria style arrangements. The three cruisers were completed between 1959 and 1961.

Tiger and her sisters had only relatively short careers as conventional cruisers. Early in 1964 it was decided that all three ships would be converted to specialist helicopter cruisers. *Blake* was the first to enter dockyard hands for the reconstruction work to begin. The conversion involved extensive changes to the ships aft of the funnels, with the 6-inch turret in 'X' position being removed to make space for a helicopter flight deck and hangar. It was originally intended to retain all three 3in gun mountings. However, a need to extend the hangar forward to house the new larger Sea King

Lion on completion displayed a very different appearance to that originally intended. The different primary and secondary armament to that of her immediate predecessors is very noticeable.

The revised bridge and lattice foremast can be clearly seen in this photograph of *Newcastle* in May 1954.

helicopter in place of the originally-intended Wessex saw two of these being replaced by more compact Seacat surface-to-air missile launchers.

Blake's modernisation took far longer and cost much more than initially envisaged. Completion of the work was further delayed by two fires. Entering dockyard hands in April 1965, it was only in 1969 that *Blake* returned to the operational fleet. One of her first duties was to carry out landing trials of the Harrier jump jet on board her helicopter deck, demonstrating the inherent potential of the revised design. *Tiger* followed *Blake* into dockyard hands, being recommissioned in 1972. The cost of the work was over £13 million, more than she had originally cost to complete. Unsurprisingly, *Lion*'s proposed modernisation was cancelled, and she was ultimately sold for scrap in 1975.

In April–May 1950, the Admiralty agreed a programme of cruiser conversions, which included the modernisation of *Belfast*, *Glasgow* and *Liverpool*, with the other three *Southampton* class, together with *Newfoundland*, *Superb* and *Swiftsure*, receiving 'large repairs'.

SOUTHAMPTON CLASS

Birmingham. During her 'large repair' at Portsmouth from July 1950 to May 1952, *Birmingham* received new bridgework, a lattice foremast and air conditioning, rendering her suitable for service in the Far East. To control the 4in AA armament, she was given two MRS6 high angle directors at the corners of the former aircraft hangar. The Type 281 radar was upgraded to the more powerful Type 960, although the antenna on the mainmast remained the same. Types 277 and 293 were upgraded. Her armament now consisted of three triple 6in turrets, four twin 4in turrets and six twin Bofors RP50 Mk 5 and six single Bofors Mk 7 40mm guns.

Newcastle. Work started on *Newcastle*'s 'large repair' at Devonport in May 1950, with the work completing in April 1952. Changes were similar to those of *Birmingham* and included a new bridge, a lattice foremast, revised sensors and fire control systems, and the new close-in anti-aircraft outfit of 18 40mm Bofors guns.

Sheffield. *Sheffield* received her 'large repair' at Chatham between November 1949 and March 1951. The work was only limited, retaining the Mk IV HACS for control of the secondary armament, the Mk VII quadruple pom-poms, and the Type 281 air-warning radar. The other AA armament was four twin Mk V and ten single Mk 7 40mm Bofors. A small lattice mast was constructed in front of the foremast to accommodate the intended larger Outfit ANU for the upgraded Type 277 radar (Type 277Q), but Outfit AUK was retained.

From January 1956 to June 1957, *Sheffield* received an upgrade to her armament, again at Chatham. Her bridge was enclosed, accommodation improved and a pre-wetting system installed. The foremast was changed to a lattice mast, which incorporated the previous small lattice mast. MRS6 was installed instead of the Mk IV HACS, radar Type 281 was replaced by Type 960, and Type 277 was upgraded. Her

Belfast in company with an American vessel in May 1952.

final light anti-aircraft outfit consisted of 8 twin Bofors RP50 Mk 5 and 2 single Bofors Mk 7.

Glasgow. *Glasgow* was refitted in 1948 and again, at Chatham, in 1951. Her modernisation was planned for 1956–57, but cancelled in late 1952. She retained her tripod foremast until decommissioned and scrapped.

GLOUCESTER CLASS

Liverpool. *Liverpool* spent seven years in the Mediterranean from October 1945 to April 1952. Her modernisation was planned for 1955–56, but, like *Glasgow*, these plans were scrapped in 1952.

EDINBURGH CLASS

Belfast. *Belfast* underwent a major refit at Portsmouth between October 1947 and October 1948, during which the deckhouses were enlarged where two 4in mountings had been removed. She then had an extended refit at Devonport between January 1956 and May 1959. An enclosed bridge was fitted together with an airtight citadel and pre-wetting facilities to combat nuclear fallout. Accommodation standards were improved throughout, and navigational aids were updated. The torpedo tubes were removed, and the weather deck plated in to just abaft the forward 4in mountings. Inflatable liferafts were also fitted.

In 1967, efforts were initiated to avert *Belfast*'s expected scrapping and to preserve her as a museum ship. In 1971, however, the government decided against preservation, prompting the formation of the private HMS *Belfast* Trust to campaign for her preservation. The efforts of the Trust were successful, and the government transferred the ship to the Trust in July 1971. Brought to London, she was moored on the River Thames near Tower Bridge. Opened to the public in October 1971, *Belfast* became part of the Imperial War Museum in 1978.

FIJI CLASS

Bermuda. *Bermuda* was refitted at Chatham Dockyard from October 1947 to May 1948. She later received an extensive refit at Palmers, Hebburn, which lasted from November 1956 until October 1957. During this period she was modernised, her bridge being enclosed, her secondary arma-

Gambia at Gibraltar in 1960.

Kenya in April 1956.

ment fitted with radar control and her tertiary armament became seven twin 40mm guns. Towards the end of her career three of these twin 40mm guns were landed.

Gambia. On return to Devonport in March 1946 *Gambia* underwent a refit. The opportunity was taken to remove her 'X' turret and modernise her light anti-aircraft armament. She was then armed with three triple 6in, four twin 4in, five twin and two single 40mm and two sets of torpedo tubes. She reverted to Royal Naval service on 1 July 1946 and her refit completed in September.

She was modernised at Rosyth from March 1956 to April 1957, with an enclosed bridge and radar control for her secondary armament. Her tertiary armament was updated and then comprised a uniform

HMCS *Quebec* in October 1952. Note the size and location of the pennant number.

HMCS *Ontario* in January 1954. Note the many changes to her secondary armament and the pennant number.

seven twin 40mm guns. Her torpedo tubes were landed. She then commissioned on 1 May 1957 and joined the Home Fleet at Invergordon.

Nigeria. *Nigeria* survived the war and continued in service with the Royal Navy, as the only 'Colony' class cruiser retaining four triple 6in turrets, 'X' turret finally being removed in 1954. In 1954 she was sold to India and underwent reconstruction, largely on the pattern of the rebuild of *Newfoundland*. In August 1957 she was commissioned into the Indian Navy, who renamed her *Mysore*. During her time with the Indian Navy, she collided with the destroyer *Hogue*, severely damaging *Hogue*'s bow. *Mysore* was in service for a further 28 years, during which time she had two more collisions, and served as a cadet training ship for ten years, before she was decommissioned in August 1985.

Mauritius. *Mauritius* was refitted at Cammell-Laird's between February 1945 and March 1946. She then served in the Mediterranean, returning to the UK in 1948. After a spell in reserve and in refit, she recommissioned in 1949 and returned to the Mediterranean, until she returned to Chatham in December 1951. *Mauritius* then went into refit for several months, before being placed in reserve in 1952 and remained there until 1965.

Kenya. At the end of the war, *Kenya* underwent a refit at Sheerness, the work lasting until September 1946. At this time her close-range armament consisted of eight single and five twin 40mm mountings. She underwent a brief refit before the Korean War, receiving another refit after the war, at Rosyth, in 1954–55, during which her 4in guns were converted to radar control. She then had two twin 40mm Mk V mountings in place of 'X' turret, one on the aft end of each hangar deck, and one amidships aft of the second funnel. She also had six single 40mm mountings.

Jamaica. *Jamaica* received refits at Devonport in 1948, at Singapore from October 1950 to January 1951, and again at Portsmouth during 1954. From August 1955 to April 1956, she underwent an extended refit at Chatham, during which she received an enclosed bridge. At the end of the refit, her close-range armament comprised five twin Mk V, two single Mk VII, and six single Mk III 40mm mountings.

UGANDA CLASS

Ceylon. *Ceylon* started a long refit in October 1954, which lasted until 1956. During this period she was modernised with radar control for her 4in guns, and given a tertiary armament of five twin and eight single 40mm guns. She was given an enclosed bridge and fitted with a lattice foremast. She recommissioned on 11 September 1956 to serve in the Home Fleet.

Uganda. Having transferred to the Royal Canadian Navy in October 1944, she entered RCN reserve in August 1947. In preparation for the Korean War, she started modernisation at Esquimalt in August 1951. She recommissioned in January 1952 as HMCS *Quebec*. Her close-range armament in Canadian service comprised two quadruple 40mm and six twin 20mm mountings.

Newfoundland. *Newfoundland* received two brief refits in 1946, at Sydney and Hong Kong, returning to Plymouth in December, where she received yet another refit, before reducing to reserve. She was modernised at Devonport Dockyard in 1950–52, when she received a new, but not enclosed, bridge. She did receive two lattice masts and was fitted with MRS6 for control of the secondary armament. At this time, she had five twin and two single 40mm mountings. Her torpedo tubes were removed. Refitted at Singapore from May to July 1955, she was involved in the Suez crisis, and returned to Portsmouth in June 1959, reducing to reserve.

In late 1959, *Newfoundland* was sold to Peru, being renamed *Almirante Grau*.

MINOTAUR CLASS

Ontario. Ontario was one of the vessels representing Canada at the naval review for Her Majesty Queen Elizabeth's Coronation in June 1953. She spent the remainder of her career as a training ship, and was paid off on 15 October 1958.

Swiftsure. In 1953 *Swiftsure* was badly damaged in a collision with the destroyer *Diamond* and paid off in 1955 for refit and modernisation. This work was never completed for reasons of economy.

Superb. Plans for *Superb*'s modernisation were abandoned after the 1957 defence review. Although *Superb* was the latest of the line of 6in gun cruisers to be completed, she was also one of the first of this type to be broken up.

HMS *Sheffield*, 1941

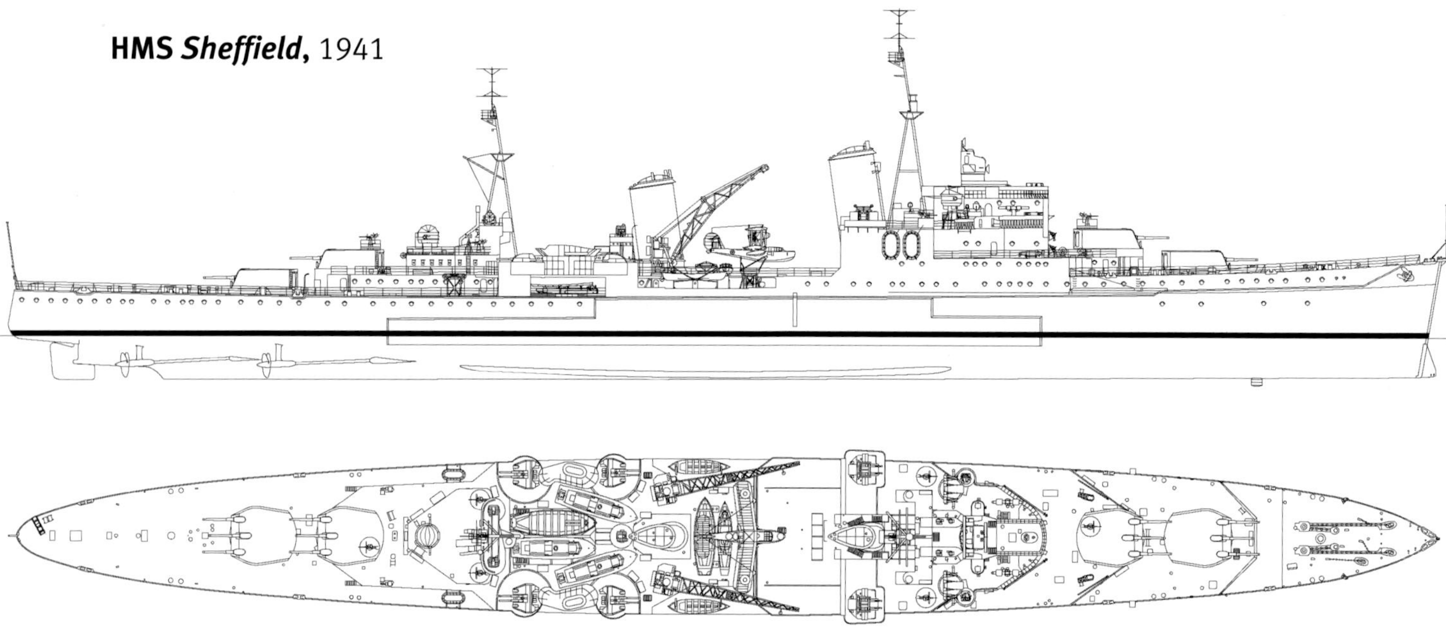

HMS *Gloucester*, 1941

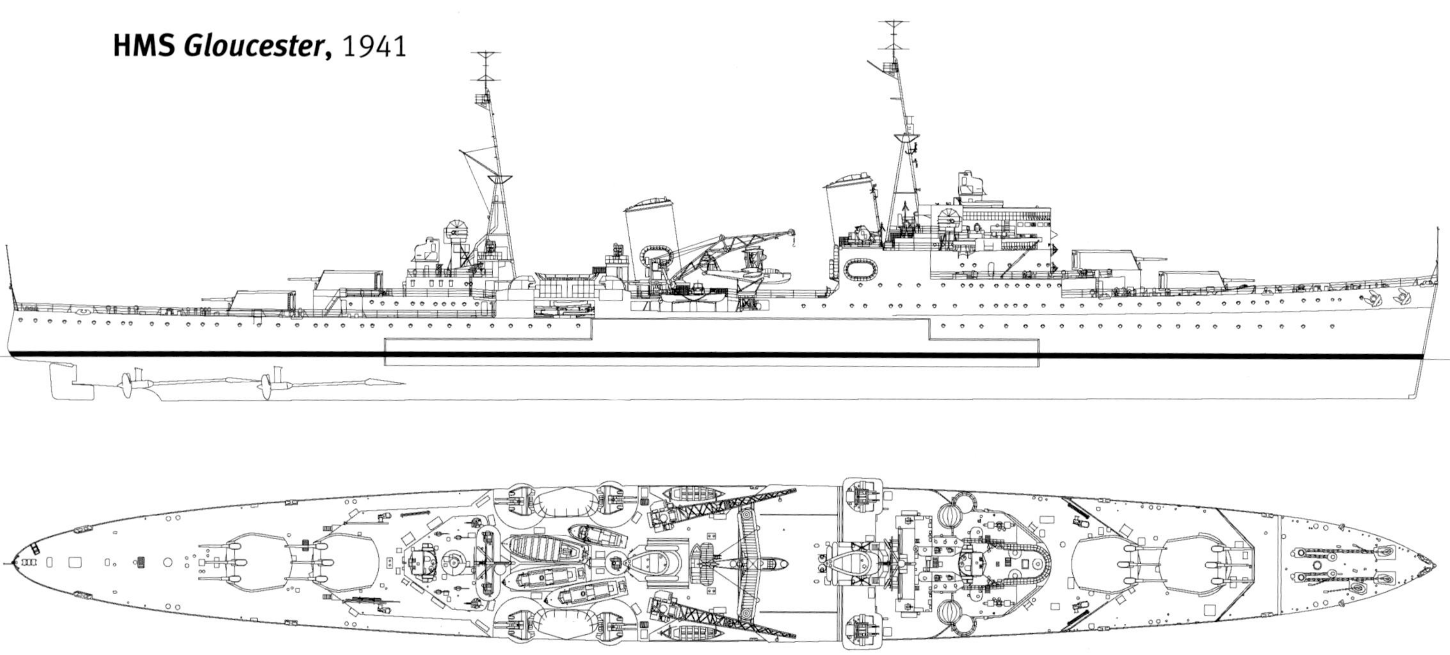

HMS *Manchester*, 1942

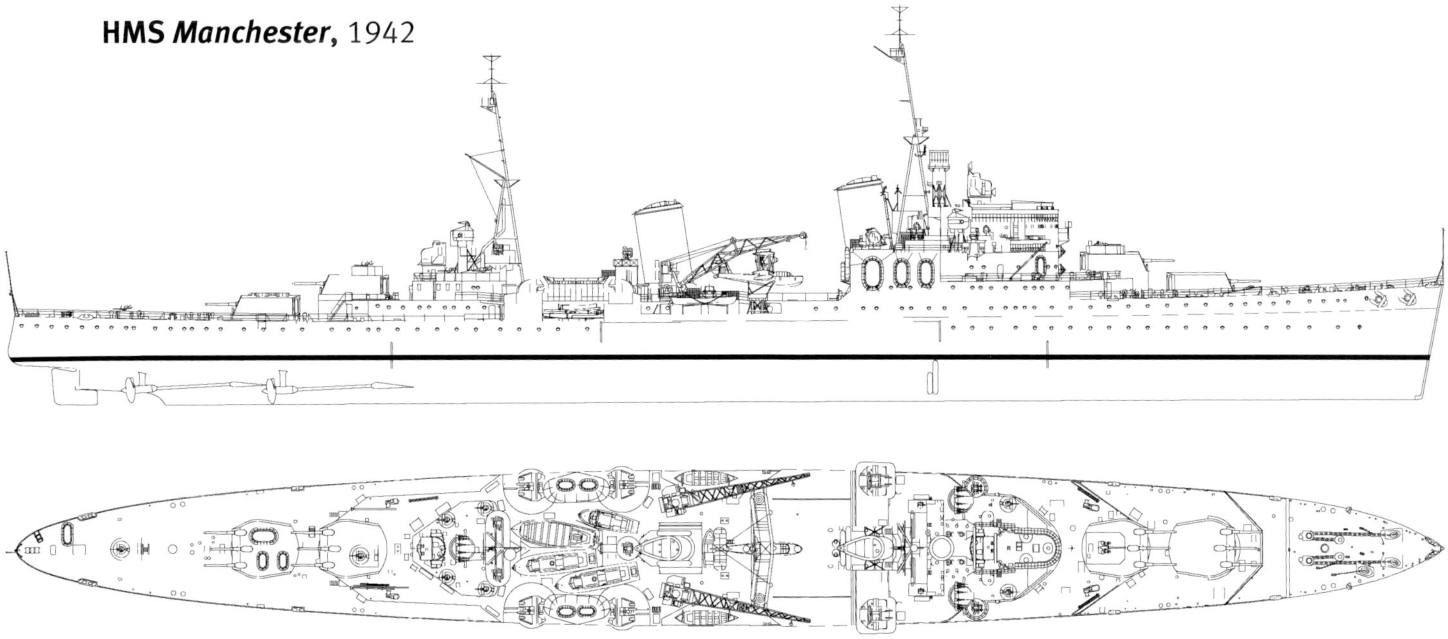

HMS *Edinburgh*, 1939

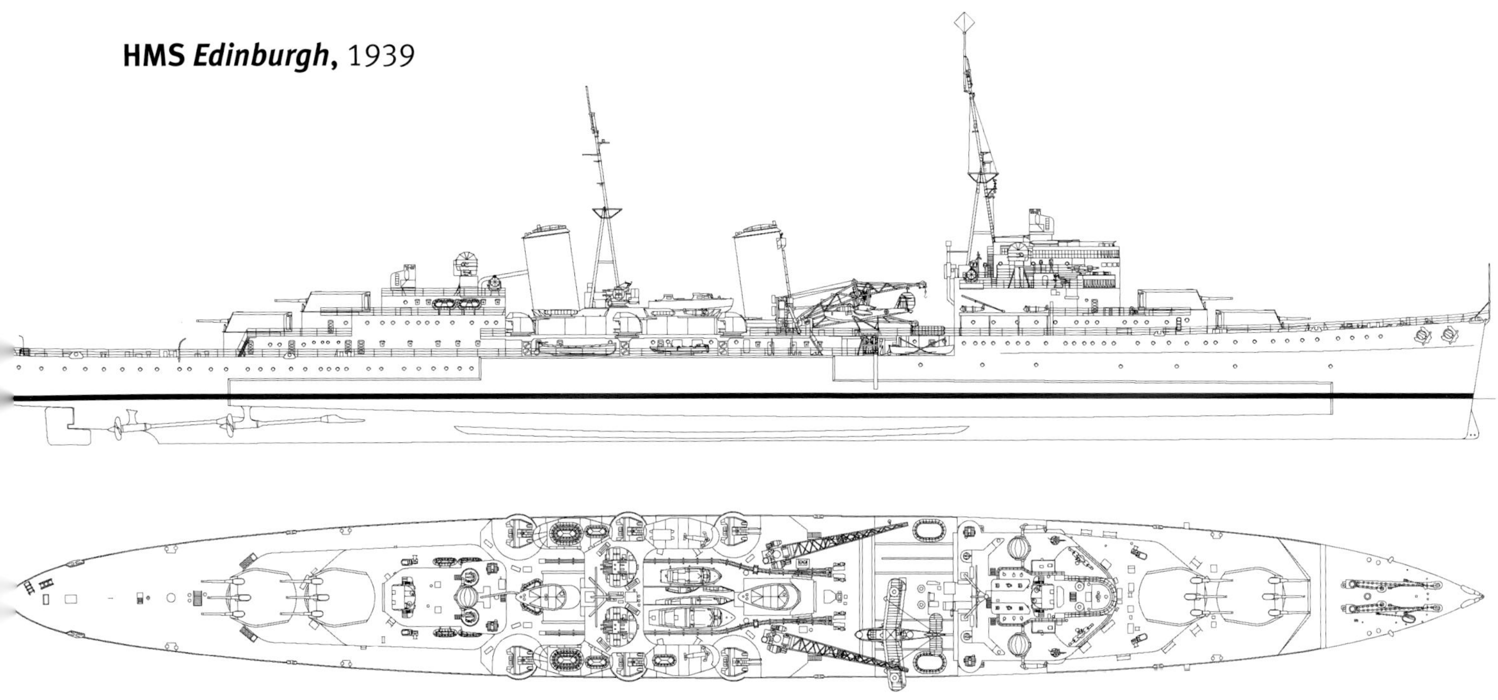

HMS *Edinburgh*, 1942

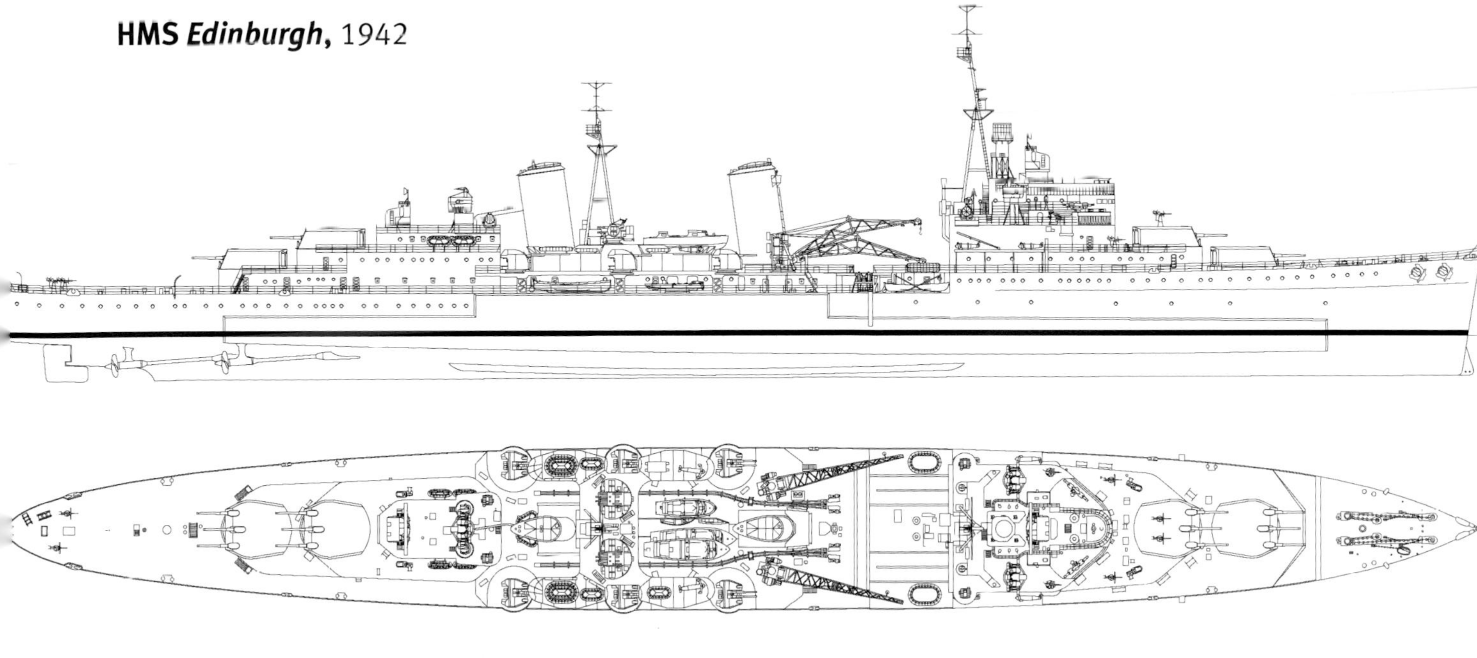

HMS *Gambia*, 1942

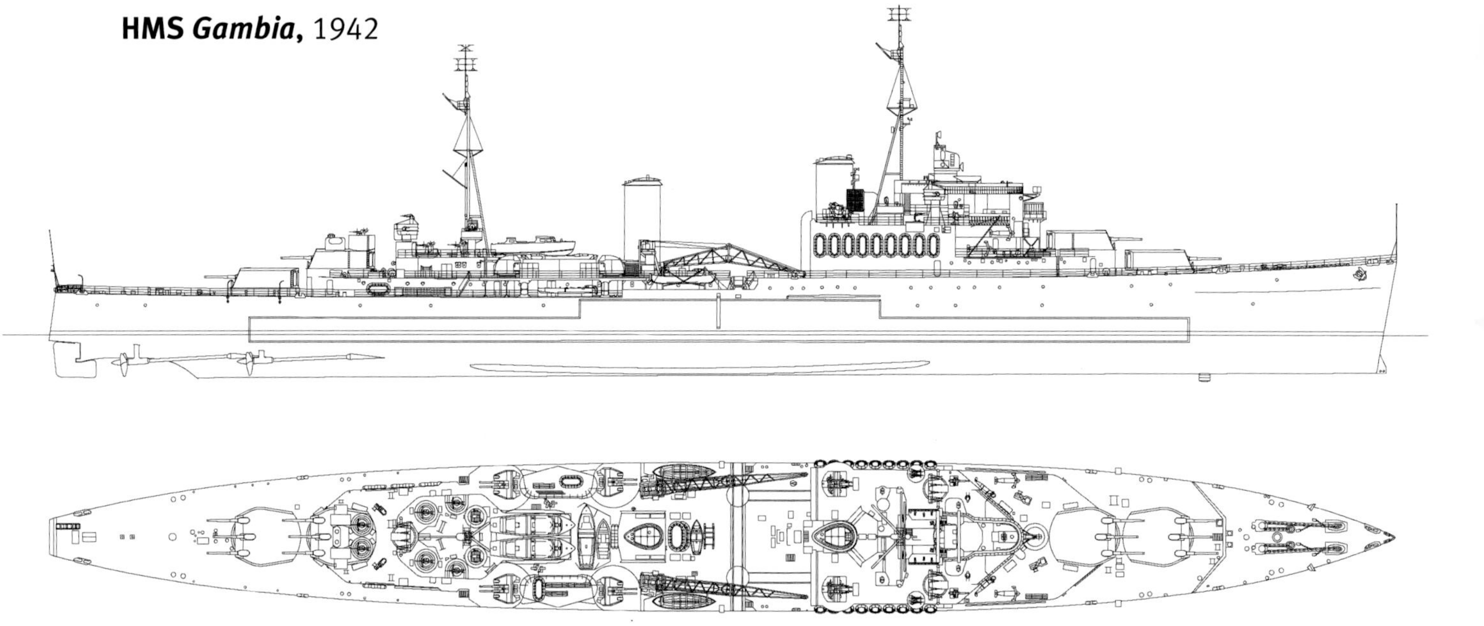

HMS *Mauritius*, 1942

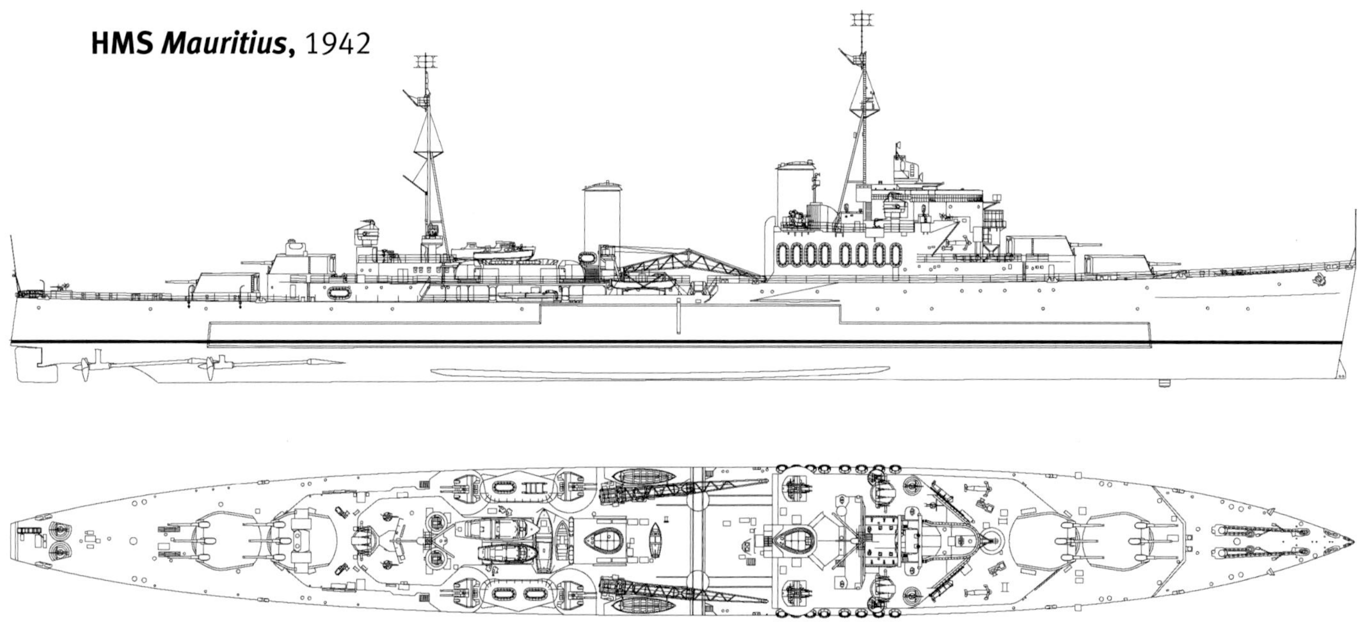

HMS *Ceylon*, 1943

HMS *Belfast*, 1959

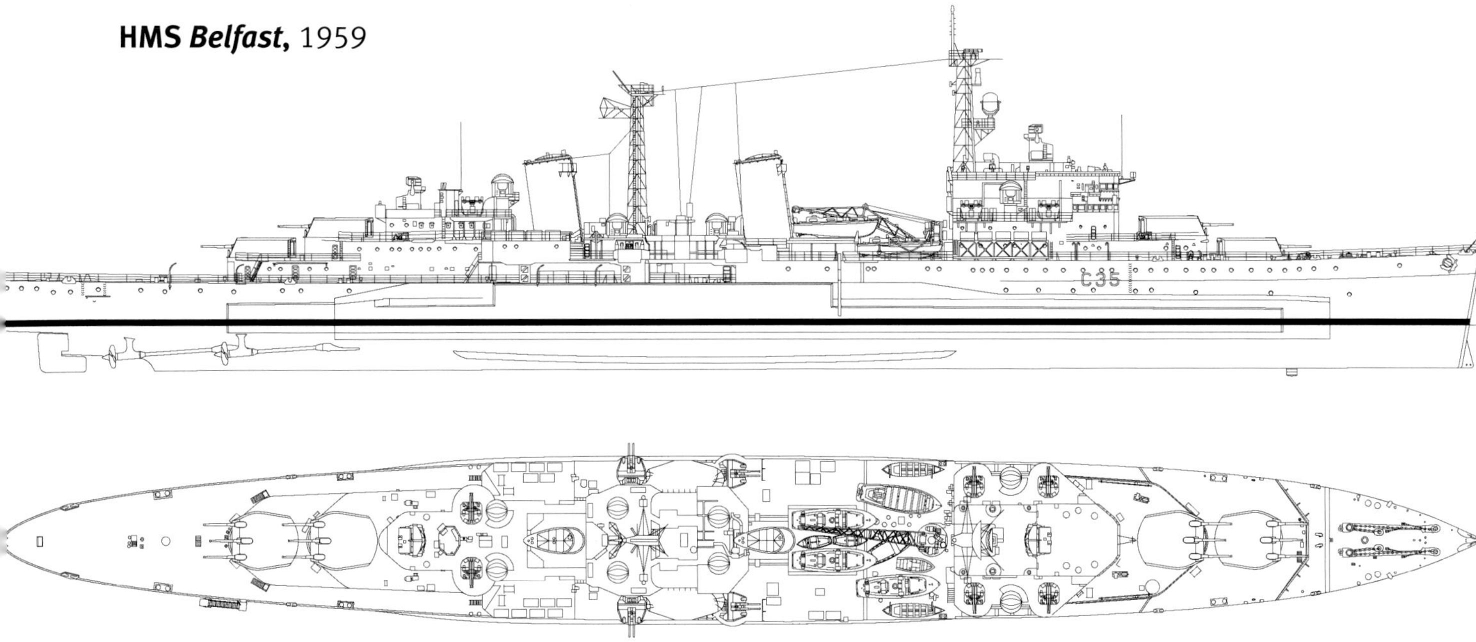

HMS *Tiger*, 1959

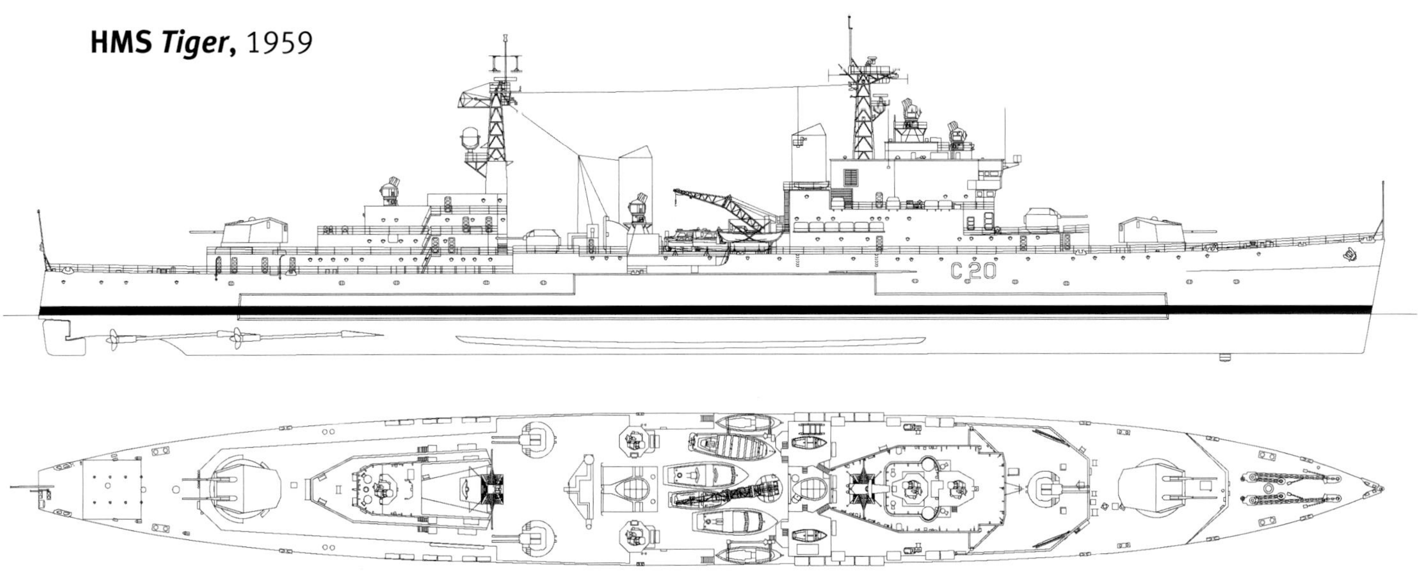

HMS *Tiger*, 1969

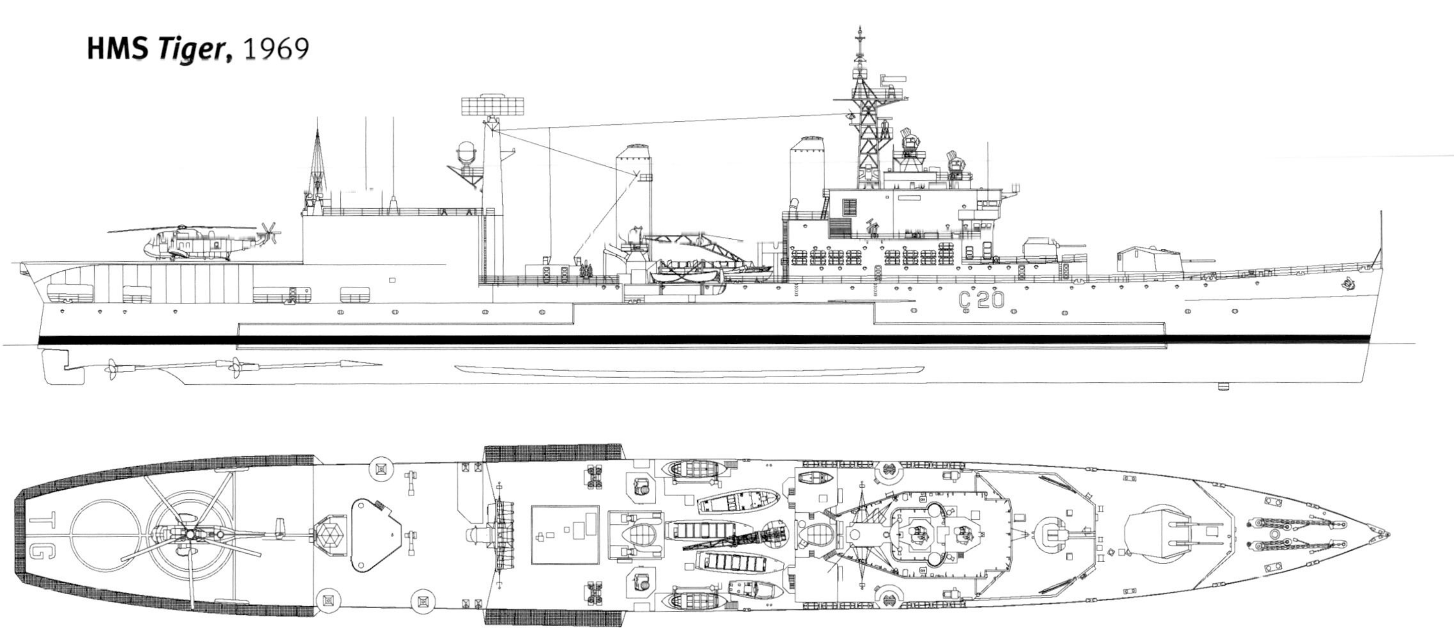

Selected References

BIBLIOGRAPHY

British & Commonwealth Warship Camouflage of WWII, Volume 3, by Malcolm Wright (Seaforth Publishing, 2016)
British Cruisers of World War Two, by Alan Raven and John Roberts (Arms and Armour Press, 1980)
British Cruisers: Two World Wars and After, by Norman Friedman (Seaforth Publishing, 2010)
British Fiji Class Cruisers and their Derivatives, by Conrad Waters (Seaforth Publishing, 2024)
British Town Class Cruisers, by Conrad Waters (Seaforth Publishing, 2019)
British Warships 1939-1945, Volume 1, edited by D K Brown (Conway Maritime Press, 1995)
British Warships of the Second World War, by Alan Raven and John Roberts (Conway Maritime Press, 1971)
British Warships, by John Roberts (Chatham Publishing, 2000)
Conway's All the World's Fighting Ships, 1922–1946, edited by Roger Chesneau (Conway Maritime Press Ltd, 1980)
Cruiser Birmingham detailed in the original builders' plans, by Conrad Waters (Seaforth Publishing, 2018)
HMNZS Gambia, by Slawomir Brzeziński (Profile Morskie 131, 2013)
HMS Belfast, by John Wingate (Profile Publications Ltd, 1972)
HMS Belfast, by Slawomir Brzeziński (Profile Morskie 10, 1998)
HMS Swiftsure, by Piotr Wiśniewski & Slawomir Brzeziński (Profile Morskie 42)
HMS Trinidad, by Slawomir Brzeziński (Profile Morskie 130, 2013)
Naval Weapons of World War Two, by John Campbell (Conway Maritime Press, 1985)
The Cruiser Belfast (Anatomy of the Ship series), by Ross Watton (Conway Maritime Press, 1985)
The Modern Cruiser, by Robert C Stern (Seaforth Publishing, 2020)
Town Class Cruisers, by Alan Raven and John Roberts (Bivouac Books Ltd, 1975)
Warships Perspectives – Royal Navy Camouflage (4 volumes), by Alan Raven (WR Press Inc, 2000–2003)

MODELLING WEBSITES

https://blackcatmodels.eu – French manufacturer of resin kits and 3D printed accessories.
https://micromaster.co.nz – New Zealand manufacturer of 3D printed parts at many scales.
https://www.atlanticmodels.net – UK manufacturer of resin kits and etched brass detail sets, including many kits previously produced by White Ensign Models (UK).
www.larsenal.com – French manufacturer of resin kits and accessories.
www.navis-neptun.de – German manufacturer of high-quality white metal models at 1:1250 scale.
www.starling-models.co.uk – UK manufacturer of resin kits and etched brass detail sets, and supplier of a wide range of plastic and resin kits and accessories from international manufacturers.
www.tomsmodelworks.com – US manufacturer of photo-etch sheets.
www.whiteensignmodels.com – US manufacturer of photo-etch sheets.

The overhead view of *Blake* clearly illustrates the extent of the modification required to produce a suitable flightdeck, and the size of the hangar.